STEPPING STONES OF THE STEWARD

LIBRARY OF CHRISTIAN STEWARDSHIP

*Stewardship in Contemporary Theology. T. K. Thompson, editor. New York: Association Press, 1960.

*Christian Stewardship and Ecumenical Confrontation. T. K. Thompson, editor. New York: Dept. of Stewardship & Benevolence, National Council of Churches, 1961.

*Stewardship in Mission. Winburn T. Thomas, editor. Englewood Cliffs: Prentice-Hall, 1964.

*Handbook of Stewardship Procedures. T. K. Thompson. Englewood Cliffs: Prentice-Hall, 1964.

*The Christian Meaning of Money. Otto A. Piper. Englewood Cliffs: Prentice-Hall, 1965.

*Stewardship Illustrations. T. K. Thompson, editor. Englewood Cliffs: Prentice-Hall, 1965.

*Stewardship in Contemporary Life. T. K. Thompson, editor. New York: Association Press, 1965.

*Why People Give. Martin E. Carlson. New York: Council Press, 1968.

*Punctured Preconceptions. Douglas W. Johnson and George W. Cornell. New York: Friendship Press, 1972.

The Steward: A Biblical Symbol Come of Age. Douglas John Hall. New York: Friendship Press, 1982.

Christian Mission: The Stewardship of Life in the Kingdom of Death. Douglas John Hall. New York: Friendship Press, 1985.

Teaching and Preaching Stewardship: An Anthology. Nordan C. Murphy, editor. New York: Friendship Press, 1985.

Imaging God: Dominion as Stewardship. Douglas John Hall. Grand Rapids: Eerdmans and New York: Friendship Press, 1986.

Public Theology and Political Economy: Christian Stewardship in Modern Society. Max L. Stackhouse. Grand Rapids: Eerdmans, 1987.

The Stewardship of Life in the Kingdom of Death. Douglas John Hall. Grand Rapids: Eerdmans, 1988 (revised edition of Christian Mission).

Stepping Stones of the Steward. Ronald E. Vallet. Grand Rapids: Eerdmans, 1989.

*Title is out of print

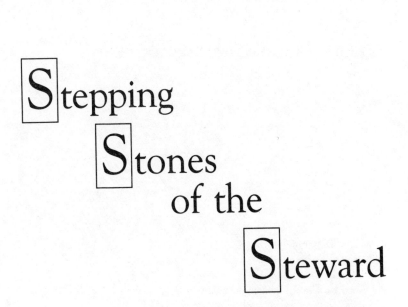

Stepping Stones of the Steward

by

Ronald E. Vallet

WILLIAM B. EERDMANS PUBLISHING COMPANY
GRAND RAPIDS, MICHIGAN

Published by Wm. B. Eerdmans Publishing Co.,
255 Jefferson Ave. S.E., Grand Rapids, Mich. 49503

Printed in the United States of America
This book is printed on permanent, durable acid-free paper

Library of Congress Cataloging-in-Publication Data

Vallet, Ronald E., 1929–
    Stepping stones of the steward / by Ronald E. Vallet.
      p.   cm.
    ISBN 0-8028-0464-0
    1. Stewardship, Christian. 2. Christian giving.
    3. Jesus Christ—Parables. I. Title.
    BV772.V26   1989
    248'.6—dc20   89-39254
                                          CIP

Unless otherwise indicated, Scripture quotations in this publication are from
the Revised Standard Version of the Bible, copyright 1946, 1952, 1971 by the
Division of Christian Education of the National Council of the Churches of
Christ in the USA, and used by permission.

To My Parents

Richard Everett Vallet
and
Angela Hicks Vallet

*Early and Faithful Guides on My Journey
as a Steward*

Contents

Preface

My father died on October 1, 1981. A few days after that date, Nancy Cook, a member of a church I had served as pastor, gave me the chrysalis spun by a monarch caterpillar as it left the larval stage and entered the pupa stage in preparation for its future life as a monarch butterfly. That chrysalis was, and is, for me a gift to be treasured. In the note that accompanied the chrysalis, she described how the monarch butterfly had emerged in full, shining radiance on October 1.

Her note described her feelings as she placed the butterfly in the garden to start its homeward journey:

> I felt sad in a way to have to let him go, such brilliant contrast of black and orange as he climbed out onto my finger. A minute part of God's glorious creation. Yet I knew I must; and you too will find comfort and joy in the golden memories of the life you shared with your father. . . .

Over the past several years, I have read, thought, and written about understanding the life of the Christian as a journey. Movement, change, growth, and development are to be expected and encouraged in our pilgrimages. In the journey, faith is acquired, sustained, strengthened, and deepened within a community of faith. The journey has become a powerful metaphor of the Christian life for me.

At the same time I was becoming sensitized to the image of steward as embodying the identity of the Christian. This, combined with the power of Jesus' parables, led me to conceive and then to write this book on the journey of the Christian steward, with a focus on Jesus' parables.

I am grateful to World Mission Support of American Baptist Churches in the U.S.A. and its executive director, Richard E. Rusbuldt, for both the opportunity and the encouragement to pursue this endeavor while a member of that staff.

Special thanks go to my wife, Rose Marie, who provided encouragement and valuable feedback, and help in the task of proofreading. My gratitude also goes to those friends who accepted my invitation to read and critique a draft version of this work. They are: Allan W. Anderson, Connie L. Burk, Ellen H. G. Culpepper, Catherine S. Edginton, Norma W. Gaskill, Floyd R. Harbold, Calvin L. Porter, Richard E. Rusbuldt, Dorothy R. Stewart, Howard O. Washburn, and Carol S. Willard.

I hope that these reflections on the journey of the Christian steward will be useful to pastors and lay members of congregations who are seeking to explore new dimensions in their journey. Questions and suggestions for individual reflection and action have been placed at the end of each chapter. The study guide at the end of the book is included to encourage and enable those who wish to study the book in a small-group setting.

Gilbertsville, Pennsylvania   Ronald E. Vallet
January 1989

Introduction

Understandings of Stewardship

My first memory of hearing about stewardship in the church, though I doubt that it was labeled stewardship, was hearing the pastor and my Sunday School teacher stress the importance of tithing. By the time I was ten years old, I had heard the word "tithing" scores of times. Whenever God gave me any income, I was taught, I was expected to calculate what 10% of that income was and to give it to the church. This was an absolute requirement. God expected it and I must do it. While I was told that the tithes of the people enabled the church to carry out its ministry and send missionaries to foreign lands, the stress was placed on the specific obligation of each person to give 10% of his or her income. In fact, I remember the preacher once saying that, even if the money I gave were burned and never used, it was still my obligation to give it to the church. Tithing was a requirement! When I got my 50 cents allowance each Saturday, I faithfully placed a nickel in the offering plate on Sunday.

During my teen years, I learned the word "stewardship," and was taught that God wanted not only 10% of my income, but also the giving of my time and talent. This was presented as a requirement as well. I was taught to be sure that 10% of my waking hours each week were used in the work of the church. During those years, my concept of stewardship was limited to the "Three T's": time, talent, and treasure.

In seminary, stewardship was presented within the context of church administration. In short, it was related to the raising of funds to underwrite the church's budget and the recruitment of volunteers to fill the various offices and positions in the church's organizational structure. Rarely was stewardship related to theological considerations. Lip service was given to statements such as, "We give because God first gave to us," but there was no serious wrestling with stewardship as a biblical and theological concept. Stewardship was something one did; it was not a matter of identity for the Christian.

By this time I had had presented to me *two quite different views of stewardship:*

1. giving as a requirement placed upon the Christian for the sake of that individual and
2. giving as a practical matter to support the work of the church and its mission.

At the present time, it is this latter view that is the prevailing mind-set of the mainline churches of North America. John H. Westerhoff III described that mind-set in these words:

> Stewardship typically has been turned into a yearly campaign for funds and an attempt to get people to devote their service to the church by teaching in the church school, singing in the choir, being on the vestry, or assisting in the liturgy. A yearly pledge of time, talent, and money, based upon programmatic budgetary needs to run an institution, is a strange understanding of stewardship.[1]

Douglas John Hall, who has helped North Americans gain a new sense of the richness of holistic stewardship, wrote blunt-

---

1. John H. Westerhoff III, *Building God's People in a Materialistic Society* (New York: Seabury Press, 1983), p. 23.

ly about the extent to which the word "steward" has suffered from current stewardship practices in the churches:

> For many churchgoers, including clergy, the term [steward] has a decidedly distasteful connotation. It at once conjures up the horrors of every-person visitations, building projects, financial campaigns, and the seemingly incessant harping of the churches for more money. Ministers cringe at the mention of Stewardship Sundays: must they really lower themselves to the status of fund-raiser once more? Must they again play the role of a Tetzel?[2]

Thoughtful church leaders are no longer content to accept such a restricted definition and practice of stewardship.

The concept of stewardship as purely functional or as a means to an end is coming under increasingly sharp attack by theologians. A consensus is emerging that stewardship is not simply a means to fund a noble end. To say that stewardship exists to facilitate the mission of the church is inadequate.

To say that the Church of Jesus Christ is called *to be a steward of God's mission* can mark the beginning of a new understanding. *As we realize that our participation in mission grows out of our identity as Christian stewards, we will be adequately motivated to participate in the mission.*

While the church engages in God's mission, it is the identity of the Christian (and the church) as steward that is the more fundamental category. Participation in mission finds its rootage in and grows out of stewardship. Mission is what God calls us to do because we are stewards. Our identity is "steward." The task to which God calls us is "mission." As that understanding takes hold, funding the mission will no longer be a major concern or problem.

To continue the prevailing stewardship practices of most North American churches, with their narrowed concept of stewardship, is to lose a holistic understanding of the life of faith. On the other hand, a return to a legalism such as I experienced

2. Douglas John Hall, *The Steward: A Biblical Symbol Come of Age* (New York: Friendship Press, 1982), p. 6.

in my childhood carries its own dangers. To present tithing as a legal requirement may destroy the spirit of gratitude and replace it with a cold, calculating, mathematical formula.

In the Bible, the steward is depicted as a person who is given the responsibility of managing something belonging to someone else. The steward is thus responsible to the owner. At the same time, the steward is not simply a passive caretaker of what has been entrusted to him or her. The steward is a full representative of the owner. Hall described these two realities as the two poles of stewardship:

> One pole—the positive one, if you like—is the close identification of the steward with his master: the steward is . . . almost the representative or vicar of his lord, though he is only a servant. The other (negative) pole is the insistence that the steward is not, after all, the owner; he is accountable to his lord, and he will be deprived of his authority unless he upholds in his actions and attitudes the authority of this Other whom he is allowed and commanded to represent.[3]

As I have explored the dimensions of what it means to be a Christian steward, I have become increasingly convinced that to envision one's primary identity as a steward can represent a summing up of the Christian life.

An excellent summary statement about stewardship was given by Westerhoff:

> Stewardship is nothing less than a complete life-style, a total accountability and responsibility before God. Stewardship is what we do after we say we believe, that is, after we give our love, loyalty, and trust to God, from whom each and every aspect of our lives comes as a gift. As members of God's household, we are subject to God's economy or stewardship, that is, God's plan to reconcile the whole world and bring creation to its proper end.[4]

3. Ibid., p. 19.
4. Westerhoff, *Building God's People in a Materialistic Society*, p. 15.

Theological Understandings

In exploring the dimensions of what it means to be a Christian steward, certain theological understandings, theological lenses, if you will, are helpful. These three metaphors have informed and guided my exploration:

(1) *God as Creator and Owner.* God created all things (Gen. 1:1). As part of the process of creation, God created human beings in the image of God and gave them particular responsibilities in relationship to the earth (Gen. 1:27-30). That which God created is owned by God: "The earth is the LORD'S and the fulness thereof. . ." (Ps. 24:1). God, therefore, may be thought of and described as Creator and Owner.

(2) *Jesus Christ as Chief Steward.* When sin entered, God established a new covenant through Jesus Christ. Paul referred to God as "He who did not spare his own Son but gave him up for us all" (Rom. 8:32) and described Jesus as the one "who, though he was in the form of God, did not count equality with God a thing to be grasped, but emptied himself, taking the form of a servant" (Phil. 2:6-7). Jesus Christ is presented not as owner, but as servant/steward. We are called to participate with Christ as "stewards of the mysteries of God" (1 Cor. 4:1). Since we participate as servants of Christ in the stewardship given to him, it is appropriate to refer to Christ as the Chief Steward. Our relationship to Christ is to acknowledge him as "Lord Jesus Christ" (Phil. 2:10-11), even as we participate with him in stewarding the mysteries of God. And what are the "mysteries of God"? In short, they are God's purpose and plan for the world (Eph. 1:9-10). It is another way of describing God's passion for the world and its redemption (John 3:16). When viewed from this perspective, stewardship and evangelism are two sides of the same coin.

(3) *The Church as Steward.* Christians are called to be stewards; the church of Jesus Christ is also a steward. The church is a trustee/agent of God's gospel for the world. When the church acknowledges Christ as head of the church (Eph. 5:23) and

the gospel, even the powers of death cannot prevail
t (Matt. 16:16-18).

Parables, Stories, and Journey

My exploration of the dimensions of what it means to be a Christian steward has been enriched in two ways: (1) through study of the parables of Jesus and other stories and (2) by conceiving the life of a Christian as a journey. This book will look at some of the parables of Jesus in relationship to the journey of the Christian steward.

There is not one of Jesus' parables that does not have deep stewardship implications. Furthermore, the use of parables is a powerful method of communicating that can have lasting impact in the lives of individuals.

One of the appeals of a parable is that it speaks in concrete images rather than abstractions. If Jesus had communicated primarily through ideas and abstractions, few persons would have understood him. We can rejoice that Jesus used parables as his chief method of teaching.

Of course, Jesus did not originate the use of the parable for teaching purposes. The parable was a common and well-understood method of illustration among Jewish teachers.

> At its simplest the parable is a metaphor or simile drawn from nature or common life, arresting the hearer by its vividness or strangeness, and leaving the mind in sufficient doubt about its precise application to tease it into active thought.[5]

The parables of Jesus have realism because "the Kingdom of God is intrinsically like the processes of nature and of the daily life of men."[6] A well-told parable can entice the hearer to make

---

5. C. H. Dodd, *The Parables of the Kingdom*, rev. ed. (New York: Charles Scribner's Sons, 1961), p. 5.

6. Ibid., p. 10.

a judgment upon the situation being depicted and then challenge him or her to apply that judgment to the situation at hand. Witness the Old Testament story of Nathan telling David the story of the poor man's ewe lamb that was stolen by the rich man. David fell neatly into the trap and Nathan retorted, "Thou art the man" (2 Sam. 12:7, AV). Jesus often introduced his parables with the question, "What do you think?" In some ways, the parable interprets us more than we interpret the parable. The parable questions us, provokes us, and sheds light on us.

> A good parable . . . does not merely serve as an illustrative point, one that could easily be omitted from the text without being missed, but rather suddenly makes the larger intent of the text transparent. At the least it introduces new possibilities of self-understanding through its metaphor; at best it alters the consciousness of the reader.[7]

The teachings of Jesus took place during a time of crisis and had significance for the particular setting in which they were delivered. Their ultimate significance, however, goes far beyond that original setting. They can be applied to new situations that were not contemplated at the time they were first spoken.

Jewish rabbis often guide their people with stories. Christian ministers usually guide with ideas and theories. The Christian church needs to recapture the art of story telling. This would enhance ministry by facilitating communication and understanding.

The characteristics of a story make it an instrument of tremendous power. Elaine M. Ward described that power in these words:

> Taste a story,
> Touch it,
> Try it.
> Tell a story,

7. Thomas C. Oden, ed., *Parables of Kierkegaard* (Princeton: Princeton University Press, 1978), p. xv.

> Sell it,
> Buy it.
> Laugh a story,
> Feel it,
> Cry it,
> Talk with it,
> Walk with it—
> And when you know your story well,
> Go fly with it![8]

A story that uses metaphor has a power almost beyond measurement. A metaphor can be so powerful that it endures for centuries, even after its original intent and meaning have sunk into obscurity. For centuries, English-speaking children have danced in a circle, holding hands and chanting:

> Ring around a rosie!
> A pocket full of posies!
> Ashes, ashes,
> All fall down.

But how many children, or adults for that matter, know that the origin of those words can be traced to the Black Death plague in Europe?

> It is said that when children saw the telltale sign during the Black Death in the 14th century, they sang "Ring around a rosie!" That meant they saw a ring on the skin around a red spot that marked the onset of the Black Death. "A pocket full of posies" meant the flowers one carried to mask the ambient stench. The ditty ended in apocalypse: "All fall down." The Black Death eventually took off half the population of Europe.[9]

The metaphors in Jesus' parables have an enduring power. This becomes evident from the way that they put flesh on the

8. Elaine M. Ward, *Storytelling—With Stories to Tell* (Nashville: Discipleship Resources, 1981), p. 4.

9. Lance Morrow, "The Start of a Plague Mentality," *Time* 126, no. 12 (September 23, 1985): 92.

bones of the abstract term "steward." As I studied the parables, I discovered that they deal with key questions that arise in the journey of the Christian steward. I found truths expressed in vivid picture-stories that help me when I am faced with decisions in my journey as a steward.

These truths lie at the heart of what it means to be a Christian steward. This book reflects my exploration of many of Jesus' parables. For me, they have become stepping stones in the journey of a Christian steward.

A story out of the Jewish tradition has taken on great significance for me as I have considered the journey of a Christian steward.

A poor Jewish man, Eizik son of Yekel, lived in the city of Krakow. One night he dreamed that, in the far city of Prague, buried at the foot of the bridge that went across the Vltava River, was a great treasure. When he awoke the next morning, he remembered his dream but did not think too much about it because it is not that unusual to have such dreams. However, that night he had the same dream again. This continued night after night, the same dream, until ten days and nights had gone by. Finally, Eizik concluded that he had no choice but to make a journey to the far city of Prague to see if a great treasure really was buried where he had seen it in his dream.

He set out on the journey to Prague, a journey that took many days and was very difficult. As he approached the city of Prague, he saw the Vltava River, just as he had seen it in his dream. Crossing the river was a bridge, just as in his dream. He hurried to the foot of the bridge, where in his dream the treasure had been buried.

As he bent over and started to dig, he felt a hand grasp his shoulder and heard a voice say to him, "What do you think you're doing here?" It was the hand and the voice of a soldier. Poor Eizik was so startled that he could think of nothing to do except to stammer out the truth. He told the soldier of his dream and of his long journey to Prague to seek the buried treasure. On hearing the story, the soldier laughed, gave Eizik a kick, and said, "You stupid Jew, don't you know that we all have dreams like that? But it makes no sense to pay attention to them. I myself had such a dream. I dreamed that in the far city of Krakow, in the house of a poor Jew named Eizik son of Yekel, a great treasure was buried beneath the stove. Now, wouldn't I be stupid if I left my post and made a long journey to Krakow and went searching through the city looking for the house of a poor Jew named Eizik? Why, there are probably many Jews with that name." With that, he gave Eizik another kick and said, "Now, go on home!"

Eizik made the long journey back to Krakow, went to his home, moved aside the stove, and dug. There he found a great treasure of gold![10]

The treasure of gold did not lie in the far city. Instead, Eizik discovered that the treasure had been very near to him for many years. But the knowledge of the treasure involved a long and difficult journey.

An Invitation

I invite you to join with me as we explore the journey of the Christian steward. The journey may be long and difficult and may not lead you or me to a treasure of gold. The journey of the Christian steward will involve a transformation—a conversion. Such a conversion, while it must begin at some particular point, will take place over time as the journey of many steps continues. The transformation, when it occurs, will be greater than when a caterpillar becomes a beautiful butterfly. It will leave a mark, as Jacob experienced when he wrestled with God and received a new identity—Israel, the one who strives with God (Gen. 32:24-31). Douglas Meeks has reminded us that even as did Jacob, *the Christian steward will walk with a limp*—the

---

10. Adapted from Belden C. Lane, "Rabbinical Stories: A Primer on Theological Method," *Christian Century* 98, no. 41 (December 16, 1981): 1309.

evidence of having struggled with God.[11] In that journey, we will learn about a treasure far greater than gold or silver—a treasure that we hold in trust as Christian stewards, the gospel of Jesus Christ.

> This is how one should regard us,
> as servants of Christ,
> and stewards of the mysteries of God. (1 Cor. 4:1)

Questions and Suggestions for Individual Reflection and Action

NOTE: The questions and suggestions at the end of each chapter are designed for those who use the book for individual study. You are encouraged to keep a written record of your thoughts and responses and to develop a plan for your journey as a Christian steward. If you are part of a small group using *Stepping Stones of the Steward*, the Study Guide at the end of the book will be of help.

1. What were your understandings of stewardship as a child and as a youth? What is your understanding at this time in your life?

2. Write a statement that describes your present understanding of stewardship.

3. What is your response to the holistic view of stewardship presented in the Introduction?

4. What are the implications as you conceive your life as the "journey of a Christian steward"?

11. In an address by M. Douglas Meeks to the Commission on Stewardship of the National Council of the Churches of Christ in the U.S.A. in December 1985.

PART I

GAINING A SENSE OF PURPOSE

The starting point in the journey of the Christian steward is—must be—a realization of the reality of God's love. Yet it is just that—a starting point, not an ending point. Accompanying the steward's recognition of God's love is an awareness that God's love is joyful and that the steward is called to participate in that joy. As God's love becomes known, it is clear that God longs for a response from each person.

As you respond to God, you will experience God as Creator and Owner and seek to fulfill the purposes of God. In that process, consciousness of your identity as a Christian steward begins to form.

Chapter 1

Love That Just Won't Quit

Parable of the Prodigal Father   (Luke 15:11-32)

And he said, "There was a man who had two sons; and the younger of them said to his father, 'Father, give me the share of property that falls to me.' And he divided his living between them. Not many days later, the younger son gathered all he had and took his journey into a far country, and there he squandered his property in loose living. And when he had spent everything, a great famine arose in that country, and he began to be in want. So he went and joined himself to one of the citizens of that country, who sent him into his fields to feed swine. And he would gladly have fed on the pods that the swine ate; and no one gave him anything. But when he came to himself he said, 'How many of my father's hired servants have bread enough and to spare, but I perish here with hunger! I will arise and go to my father, and I will say to him, "Father, I have sinned against heaven and before you; I am no longer worthy to be called your son; treat me as one of your hired servants."' And he arose and came to his father. But while he was yet at a distance, his father saw him and had compassion, and ran and embraced him and kissed him. And the son said to him, 'Father, I have sinned against heaven and before you; I am no longer worthy to be called your son.'

But the father said to his servants, 'Bring quickly the best robe, and put it on him; and put a ring on his hand, and shoes on his feet; and bring the fatted calf and kill it, and let us eat and make merry; for this my son was dead, and is alive again; he was lost, and is found.' And they began to make merry.

"Now his elder son was in the field; and as he came and drew near to the house, he heard music and dancing. And he called one of the servants and asked what this meant. And he said to him, 'Your brother has come, and your father has killed the fatted calf, because he has received him safe and sound.' But he was angry and refused to go in. His father came out and entreated him, but he answered his father, 'Lo, these many years I have served you, and I never disobeyed your command; yet you never gave me a kid, that I might make merry with my friends. But when this son of yours came, who has devoured your living with harlots, you killed for him the fatted calf!' And he said to him, 'Son, you are always with me, and all that is mine is yours. It was fitting to make merry and be glad, for this your brother was dead, and is alive; he was lost, and is found.'"

Realizing How Much God Loves You

A basic starting point for experiencing the reality of being a Christian steward is to realize how much God loves you. The parable of the prodigal father (Luke 15:11-32) vividly depicts the breadth and the depth of God's love. "His father saw him and had compassion, and ran and embraced him and kissed him."

*　　　*　　　*

God's love is made known to human beings through personal experiences. God is not encountered in the abstract, but in specific, historical events. God is known through active involvement with people.

A Father and Two Sons

This parable of Jesus, usually called the parable of the prodigal son, could be named the parable of the *prodigal father*. The spotlight is never off the father, who is the central character in the story. The actions of the two sons stand in vivid contrast to the demonstrated love of the father. But how can we describe the father as prodigal? We can if we understand the word "prodigal" according to its primary meaning. "Prodigal" means extravagant, very generous in giving, lavish, and unrestrained. That is a good description of the father.

Why did the younger son ask for his share of the inheritance and make his way to a far country? We have usually assumed that he did so with the deliberate intention of wasting the money in loose living. But this is not necessarily so. Often Jewish younger sons ventured into the Dispersion, just as centuries later British younger sons went to the colonies and American younger sons responded to the challenge: "Go west, young man." In any event, the father, in love, gave his younger son his share of the inheritance.

17

Probably the younger son thought that he had left home for good. The money was his. He was in charge of his own life. No longer would he have to be accountable to his father. Whatever may have been the original intent of the younger son, he did in fact recklessly spend all the money he had been given. When a famine came to that country, he was reduced to feeding the swine.

His descent into despair was swift. He lost all his money; then he lost hope. In hunger and desperation he became a hired servant in that far country—at the bottom of the heap.

At the depth of his despair, he "came to himself" and decided to return home, confess his sin, and ask his father to accept him as a hired servant. The son meant to beg admission to the lowest rank of all. But he never got a chance to make his request.

Most fathers would have spurned a son returning in such disgrace. But this father was not typical. He was a father who looked down the road each day, possibly several times a day, to see if his son was returning. The scene that follows is one of the most dramatic in all literature.

When the father saw him at a distance and ran to meet him, there was no hesitation, no reluctance. Although it was considered undignified for a senior man to run, this was not a moment for dignity. It was a time for love to be demonstrated. The father recognized the gravity of his son's offense: "My son was dead and is alive again." But the offense was forgiven in a way that can only be described as extravagant. There is no doubt that the extravagance was deliberate, as the father freely forgave his younger son, treated him as an honored guest, and restored him to a position of dignity and authority in the household.

Jesus emphasized in image after image the free and absolute nature of the father's forgiveness, all in deliberate contrast to the expectation of those to whom the parable was addressed. The embrace and kiss were an immediate sign of forgiveness; the giving of a feast a sign that this was an occasion of rejoicing and celebration; the best robe (probably the father's own) a demonstration that the son was an honored guest; the ring a symbol of trusted authority; and the shoes a sign that he was a free man in the house, not a servant.

Listeners to the Parable

The viewpoint of those to whom the parable was being addressed was not ignored. Who were they? We are told in Luke 15:1-2: "Now the tax collectors and sinners were all drawing near to him. And the Pharisees and the scribes murmured, saying, 'This man receives sinners and eats with them.'" Their viewpoint is introduced on the lips of the elder son—the character in the story whom we often tend to forget.

The elder son protested in the name of a regular and seemingly quite proper concept of justice. He had spent his years "doing his duty," but at the same time he was squandering months and years of opportunity to discover the true meaning of home and sonship. How could he be expected to embrace and congratulate his brother, treating him as an honored guest?

The older brother had stayed home and behaved himself, or so it seemed. Beneath his veneer of propriety, he was a wolf in sheep's clothing. "A good man in the worst sense of the word," as Mark Twain said.[1]

Probably the older son's greatest fault was to be conscious of no fault. He was as far from his father as his younger brother had been in the far country. Like his brother, he forgot that what he had was a trust from the father. When the father heard of his older son's objections to the welcoming feast for his brother, he "came out and entreated him" to come in. This was love's entreaty, an invitation to come to the party. The older son responded by recounting his own faithful service to the father, in contrast to the behavior of his brother whom he referred to

---

1. The Mark Twain quotation is taken from David A. Redding, *The Parables He Told* (Westwood, NJ: Fleming H. Revell, 1962), p. 16. The source is not cited.

as "this son of yours." The contrast between the delight of the father and the surly attitude of the "respectable" older brother is sharp and unmistakable.

Jesus was speaking to the self-righteous "saints" of any age who begrudge God's love to others. Jesus was roundly criticized for his table fellowship with prostitutes and tax collectors. Such is a spirit of judgmentalism that says to persons who are lost and broken, "You are the way you are because you didn't work as hard as I did. It's your own fault."

Both sons had failed the father, but only one realized it. The father loved each of them in a way that was appropriate for each one. If only the older son could have loved his brother as his father did.

An ancient Jewish story reveals what can happen when there is love between brothers:

> Time before time, when the world was young, two brothers shared a field and a mill, each night dividing evenly the grain they had ground together during the day. One brother lived alone; the other had a wife and a large family. Now the single brother thought to himself one day, "It isn't really fair that we divide the grain evenly. I have only myself to care for, but my brother has children to feed." So each night he secretly took some of his grain to his brother's granary to see that he was never without. But the married brother said to himself one day, "It isn't really fair that we divide the grain evenly, because I have children to provide for me in my old age, but my brother has no one. What will he do when he is old?" So every night he secretly took some of his grain to his brother's granary. As a result, both of them always found their supply of grain mysteriously replenished each morning.
>
> Then one night they met each other halfway between their two houses, suddenly realized what had been happening, and embraced each other in love. The legend is that God witnessed their meeting and proclaimed, "This is a holy place—a place of love—and here it is that my temple shall be built." And so it was.[2]

2. Belden C. Lane, "Rabbinical Stories: A Primer on Theological Method," *Christian Century* 98, no. 41 (December 16, 1981): 1307-8.

In the parable, Jesus was revealing a new situation—a new understanding. God's love is free, unmerited, and unconditional. It is a love that just won't quit.

God's Love in This New Age

The New Testament proclaims a "new order," a "new creation," a "new world," a "new age." We live in this "new age," though we do not always grasp its full significance. The key to understanding this "new age" is to know and to experience the love of God and to live out its implications in our lives. But this is easier to say than to do.

Are we like the man described here?

> . . . a man who sat in a dark cave. The only source of light was that which filtered through the cave opening. The man was fascinated by the shadows cast upon the cave wall. The shadows, he believed, were real and represented the totality of life. There was no need to seek further. Contentedly, he watched the shadows dance across the cave wall.
>
> One day, something beckoned him to come out of the cave. He resisted, but finally gave in to curiosity. He ventured out and, to his amazement, discovered a new world; a world of light, colors, and sound, not just dark shadows on a wall. Never again would he return to darkness.[3]

Do we, after coming out of the cave and learning of a whole new world, turn back to the seeming safety and comfort of the cave? It is easy to stay with the familiar. Do we say that we want to experience God's love, yet flee from it when its intensity becomes real to us?

One indication that we are not fully appropriating the love of God comes when we are impatient and complaining—just as

3. Richard Matsushita, "A Stewardship of Service," in *Thanks*Giving: Stewardship Sermons out of the Ethnic Minority Experience, ed. J. LaVon Kincaid, Sr. (Nashville: Discipleship Resources, 1984), p. 22.

the younger son who wanted his share of the inheritance immediately or the older son who complained about the father's love for the "unworthy" son. It is easy to murmur, to complain, to say, "God, why did you let this happen to me?" When we realize the breadth and the depth of God's love, however, we will see ourselves and everything around us in the light of the "new age."

In Jesus' parable, the fall and return of the younger son led to a family crisis in which the father's love created the setting for a new and deeper reality of family life and relationships. And when Jesus proclaimed forgiveness of sins and "tax collectors and other Jews who had made themselves as Gentiles" responded in glad acceptance, Palestinian Judaism was confronted by a crisis. It was a situation in which the reality of God's love was revealed in new, decisive ways. The joys of salvation were suddenly available to those who had longed for them long and earnestly.

God's most basic characteristic is love. St. Augustine said, "God loves each one of us as if there were only one of us." It is love demonstrated in Jesus' parable as the father runs to welcome the younger son and entreats the older son to come to the party. It is love that led God to give us the greatest demonstration of love in the person of Jesus. God loved . . . God gave.

It is a love so great that it is beyond our human capacity to comprehend or to verbalize to its full extent. Yet we have the privilege of joining in the celebration of the new relationship with God and one another. These words were reportedly penciled on the wall of a narrow room of an asylum by a man said to have been demented:

> Could we with ink the ocean fill,
> And were the skies of parchment made;
> Were every stalk on earth a quill,
> And ev'ry man a scribe by trade;
> To write the love of God above
> Would drain the ocean dry;

Nor could the scroll contain the whole,
Tho' stretched from sky to sky.[4]

The Journey

In your journey as a steward, the starting point is your recognition of the reality of God's love. It reaches out to you whether you are "near" or "far." Other factors aid you in your journey as well. To experience God's love is a first step, but there is more. As we will see in the next chapter, joy comes to each person who experiences God's love. The journey of the Christian steward has many stepping stones.

Questions and Suggestions
for Individual Reflection and Action

1. What experiences in your life are brought to mind by the parable of the prodigal father?

2. What are the advantages and disadvantages of conceiving the first step in the journey of the Christian steward as a realization of the reality of God's love? Why is this not the only "stepping stone" in the Christian steward's journey?

3. What are the similarities and differences in the two brothers' relationship to their father? What does this say about how much God loves you?

4. What steps might you take in your life to enhance your realization of God's love?

4. "The Love of God" (Kansas City, MO: Lillenas Publishing Company, 1917).

Chapter 2

Joy That Endures

Parables of the Lost Sheep and the Lost Coin
(Luke 15:1-10)

Now the tax collectors and sinners were all drawing near to hear him. And the Pharisees and the scribes murmured, saying, "This man receives sinners and eats with them."

So he told them this parable: "What man of you, having a hundred sheep, if he has lost one of them, does not leave the ninety-nine in the wilderness, and go after the one which is lost, until he finds it? And when he has found it, he lays it on his shoulders, rejoicing. And when he comes home, he calls together his friends and his neighbors, saying to them, 'Rejoice with me, for I have found my sheep which was lost.' Just so, I tell you, there will be more joy in heaven over one sinner who repents than over ninety-nine righteous persons who need no repentance.

"Or what woman, having ten silver coins, if she loses one coin, does not light a lamp and sweep the house and seek diligently until she finds it? And when she has found it, she calls together her friends and neighbors, saying, 'Rejoice with me, for I have found the coin which I had lost.' Just so, I tell you, there is joy before the angels of God over one sinner who repents."

Feeling Joy in the Presence of God

A corollary of God's love is the joy you find in the presence of God. The parables of the lost sheep and the lost coin (Luke 15:1-10) have joy as the major theme. "Rejoice with me, for I have found my sheep which was lost!"

*   *   *

Charlie Brown, the leading character in the "Peanuts" comic strip series, wants very much to be liked and treated with respect. He lives in continuing hope that Lucy will like him. In one episode, Charlie Brown is lying down with his head resting on a stone as Lucy stands beside him. Charlie looks up at Lucy and asks, "If I tell you something, Lucy, will you promise not to laugh?" Lucy replies, "I promise." Charlie: "This is very personal and I don't want you to laugh." Lucy responds, "You have my solemn promise." Charlie then shares something very special to him, "Sometimes I lie awake at night listening for a voice that will cry, 'We LIKE you, Charlie Brownnnn!'" Lucy bursts forth with a boisterous, "HA HA HA HA," and Charlie is bowled over from his reclining position. Robert L. Short added this comment to that cartoon strip: "Christianity proclaims, however, that the scornful, derisive laughter of 'Lucy-fer' is not the last word; that life is not finally a cruel joke in which we are the punch lines."[1]

Experiencing Joy

Christianity is a proclamation of joy. The parable of the lost sheep is a parable of joy. Jesus used a story about a pastoral scene because sheep and shepherds were an integral part of daily life at that time. The Jewish Scriptures are filled with pastoral images.

---

1. Robert L. Short, *The Parables of Jesus* (New York: Harper & Row, 1968), p. 132.

The relationship between sheep and shepherds in Palestine was very close. Sheep in Palestine were rarely kept for killing, but for their wool. As a result, a sheep was often in the flock for up to eight or nine years. Shepherds called the sheep by name and did not walk behind them, but in front. When the flock came to a narrow place where robbers or wild beasts might be hiding, shepherds were the first to meet the danger, even risking their lives to save the sheep.

A hundred sheep were a sign of prosperity. But what kind of shepherd would leave ninety-nine sheep in an open pasture to go search for one gone astray? Was that good business? Why not cut one's losses and get on with caring about the flock? Why was one sheep important? The simple answer is that the shepherd cared about all the sheep.

A Sense of Loss

When Jesus told the parables of the lost sheep and the lost coin, he was sharing the great joy felt by the shepherd who found the lost sheep and the woman who found the lost coin. But before there was joy, there was a sense of loss. The shepherd felt the loss of the one sheep, even though he still had ninety-nine. The woman felt the loss of the one silver coin, even though she had nine remaining. The parables express "the concern which a person feels about a loss which an outsider might consider comparatively trifling, and his (or her) corresponding delight when the lost is found."[2]

While serving as pastor of a small congregation in rural upstate New York in the years before any of our children had been born, my wife and I had a dog and a cat. One day we discovered that our cat, Sputter, was missing. We searched through the house and in the yard outside. Sputter was nowhere to be

2. C. H. Dodd, *The Parables of the Kingdom*, rev. ed. (New York: Charles Scribner's Sons, 1961), p. 92.

found. Later that day we looked in nearby yards and fields, calling her name and asking other persons if they had seen our missing cat. No one had seen her. When night came, we still had not found her. The next day we continued to look, searching an even wider area. Still she was not to be found. We went to bed that second night very sad and discouraged. The third day we searched again, calling her name, but we did not find her. Later that morning, while looking out a living room window, my wife spotted Sputter—about 150 feet away, sitting on the sill inside the basement window of the house next door. What joy my wife felt and then I felt as she shared the good news with me.

The woman who lived in the house was away for several months that winter. Once or twice a week her brother stopped by to check the house. Apparently Sputter had entered the basement during one of his visits and had been locked in the cellar. After she was spotted by us, we called the brother on the phone and he came over to open the cellar door. When the door was opened, Sputter came rushing out, purring and rubbing against our legs. Her joy was evident to us, and our joy was great, too! Sputter had no economic value to us or to anyone else. But we loved her; she was special to us. When we found her, we rejoiced and others rejoiced with us.

What It Means to Be Lost

One of the key words in the two parables is the word "lost." What does it mean to be lost? The Pharisees to whom Jesus was speaking had difficulty identifying with the lost sheep. They had not thought of themselves in that condition. Does it have meaning for us?

One way in which we can experience being lost is to feel that we do not have an intimate relationship with God. This can happen if we search for a new turf of satisfaction and adventure, no longer desiring that God be a part of our lives. When this happens, we lose our direction. We feel lost, with many choices and with no clear conviction of where our lives are headed.

If we do not feel loved, we will feel lost and there will be no joy. If we do not feel that we are "special" to anyone, especially the significant people of our lives, we will feel lost. As a result, we may be in the lost condition of not even loving ourselves. The lost ache of broken relationships, misunderstandings, differences, arguments, cutting words, and sickening silences can leave us hurting and without joy.

The fear of death can hold a person captive, so that the freeing, joyful spirit of the Resurrection is not being experienced. We forget that God, in Christ, has conquered death.

Perhaps most tragic is not knowing that we are lost, as when we are insensitive to the pain of other people and are judgmental and critical. This is the lostness of self-centeredness.

Could the Pharisees and the scribes hearing the parables of the lost sheep and the lost coin conceive that a loving God would pursue someone who was lost and then rejoice when the lost was found? Another question: Can you and I?

God's Search

Jesus, the searching Shepherd, has left the ninety-nine and is searching for you and me. In the words of Pascal, "You would not be searching for me if I had not already found you." Any longing for God is because God has already drawn near.

> So long as we imagine that it is we who have to look for God, then we must often lose heart. But it is the other way about: he is looking for us. And so we can afford to recognize that very often we are not looking for God; far from it, we are in full flight from him, in high rebellion against him. And he knows that and has taken it into account. He has followed us into our own dark-

ness; there where we thought finally to escape him, we run straight into his arms.[3]

God *does* go after us. "The Hound of Heaven" by Francis Thompson describes God's relentless pursuit:

> I fled Him, down the nights and down the days;
> I fled Him, down the arches of the years;
> I fled Him, down the labyrinthine ways
> Of my own mind; and in the mist of tears
> I hid from Him, and under running laughter
> Up vistaed hopes I sped;
> And shot, precipitated,
> Adown Titanic glooms of chasmed fears.
> From those strong feet that followed,
> followed after.[4]

God is kinder than humankind. We write people off. God does not. We give up hope on someone. Not so God. God seeks out the lost and rejoices when they are found.

When the lost sheep was found, the shepherd was joyful. He anointed the cut and bruised sheep and hoisted it upon his shoulders. He strode back toward his friends and called from a distance, "Rejoice with me, for I have found my sheep which was lost." It is a picture of God carrying you and me home, and rejoicing.

Joy as a Mark of the Steward

Joy is an identifiable characteristic of the people of God, a stepping stone on the journey of the Christian steward. "The morning stars sang together, and all the sons [children] of God shouted for joy" (Job 38:7).

3. Simon Tugwell, *Prayer*, quoted by Rueben P. Job and Norman Shawchuck in *A Guide to Prayer for Ministers and Other Servants* (Nashville: Upper Room, 1983), p. 161.

4. Quoted by Lloyd John Ogilvie in *Autobiography of God* (Glendale, CA: GL Regal Books, 1979), pp. 33-34.

Our only true joy is that which comes from God through God's sharing, the joy of finding the lost. In the long run, there is no other joy than God's joy.

Communion is described as the joyful feast of the People of God. God's gift of Jesus, his death and resurrection, is joyous. Yet one of the strange paradoxes of Christian life is that we are often somber and sad when the occasion calls for us to be joyful. One of the most striking illustrations of this is the way Communion is observed in many churches. Typically, those who are leading the service do so in a hushed, subdued tone, almost as though it were a funeral service.

Actually, of course, it is the Eucharist, an occasion of thanksgiving. It is a time of joy. The words that are often used in leading Communion services remind us of this:

> Beloved, this is the joyful feast of the people of God.
> Men and women will come from east and west,
> and from north and south,
> and sit at table in the reign of God.

These words are followed by a prayer of thanksgiving. As we remember the death of Jesus, we celebrate the victory over death and the gift that God gave to each one of us.

At the Lord's Table, we can experience what it means to be a steward. For the Lord's Table is the distribution of the Lord's righteousness. And we come to the Table with a new identity— received through the transformation symbolized by Baptism.

Thomas G. Pettepiece described a Communion service that was joyous even when there seemed to be no reason for joy. The experience took place on Easter in a prison with almost 10,000 political prisoners. In that setting a score of Christian prisoners experienced the joy of celebrating Communion without bread or wine—a communion of empty hands.

> The non-Christians said: "We will help you; we will talk quietly so that you can meet." Too dense a silence would have drawn the guards' attention as surely as the lone voice of the

preacher. "We have no bread, nor water to use instead of wine." I told them, "but we will act as though we had." . . .

I held out my empty hand to the first person on my right, and placed it over his open hand, and the same with the others: "Take, eat, this is my body which is given for you; do this in remembrance of me." Afterward, all of us raised our hands to our mouths, receiving the body of Christ in silence. "Take, drink, this is the blood of Christ which was shed to seal the new covenant of God with men. Let us give thanks, sure that Christ is here with us, strengthening us."

We gave thanks to God, and finally stood up and embraced each other. A while later, . . . [a] non-Christian prisoner said to me: "You people have something special, which I would like to have." The father of . . . [a] dead girl came up to me and said: "Pastor, this was a real experience! I believe that today I discovered what faith is. Now I believe that I am on the road."[5]

The Journey

People who know that they are freed from guilt and the fear of death are joyful. Joyful people can make a radical difference in the household and economy of God. There will be no stewards without such a joyous freedom.

The faith journey of the Christian steward involves realizing God's love and experiencing the joy felt by God when the lost is found. But there is more. You are called to respond.

Questions and Suggestions
for Individual Reflection and Action

1. Recall and reflect on an experience of joy that you have felt or observed recently.

5. Thomas G. Pettepiece, *Visions of a World Hungry*, quoted by Job and Shawchuck in *A Guide to Prayer for Ministers and Other Servants*, pp. 143-44.

2. Where do you see evidences of joy in your life, in the lives of friends, of members of your congregation, and in the life of your congregation as a whole? What are the sources of that joy?

3. Why is joy an essential ingredient in the experience of the Christian steward?

4. What steps might you take to increase experiences of joy in your life and in the lives of others?

Chapter 3

Your Response to God: A Multiple Choice

Parable of the Soils   (Matthew 13:1-9)

That same day Jesus went out of the house and sat beside the sea. And great crowds gathered about him, so that he got into a boat and sat there; and the whole crowd stood on the beach. And he told them many things in parables, saying: "A sower went out to sow. And as he sowed, some seeds fell along the path, and the birds came and devoured them. Other seeds fell on rocky ground, where they had not much soil, and immediately they sprang up, since they had no depth of soil, but when the sun rose they were scorched; and since they had no root they withered away. Other seeds fell upon thorns, and the thorns grew up and choked them. Other seeds fell on good soil and brought forth grain, some a hundredfold, some sixty, some thirty. He who has ears, let him hear."

Responding to God's Overtures

God's love, as powerful as it is, needs a responsive human heart if it is to bear fruit. The parable of the soils (Matthew 13:1-9) describes different responses to the seed. "Other seeds fell on good soil and brought forth grain. . . ."

*　　　*　　　*

Listening

Business corporations spend hundreds of millions of dollars each year producing television commercials in the hope that people will watch and listen to their commercials and be persuaded to buy their products. We are bombarded with messages such as:

- "What would you do-oo-o for a Klondike bar?"
- "Don't send a wimpy bag to do a Hefty job."
- "Aren't you glad you used Dial?"
- "Kix . . . kid tested, mother approved."
- "They're one of a kind; they're Cabbage Patch Preemies. You can give them all of your love."
- "Oh what a feeling—to drive a Toyota!"

The business world knows well that most people do not listen automatically.

Yet most people mistakenly assume that listening is not difficult, that it is much easier than speaking or writing, for example. Evidence indicates otherwise. Consider the differing perceptions that persons who attend the same meeting may have. Each person will remember it differently. This can be true even in family discussions. Afterwards, one person may say to the other, "but you said. . . ," to which the other person may reply, "I didn't say that."

Active listening is an important skill that can have value in any human dialogue or relationship. Many people have benefitted from participating in workshops to develop the skills of active listening. Active listening, very briefly, can be defined as:

1. listening to what another person is saying,
2. sensing the feelings of the other person about what he or she is saying, and
3. giving that person feedback to test the accuracy of the listener's perception of what the speaker actually meant and felt.

The parable of the soils makes the point that we need to be active listeners to God as well. As part of God's creation, you and I are created with the capacity to listen to God. But how well do we listen?

Choosing and Responding

Jesus was pressed by crowds as he stood beside the Sea of Galilee and taught. He was forced to use a small fishing boat as his pulpit. From that vantage point he could see not only the crowd but also a sower sowing seed on nearby hills.

The rest of the parable is about the *soil*. The seed was all the same. But the ground into which those seeds fell was not all the same. This gave Jesus the example he needed.

Do you remember taking multiple choice tests—the kind of test where, following each question, several possible answers to the question are listed? You then mark the answer you feel is correct. This particular parable of Jesus lends itself to a multiple-choice approach.

The four kinds of soil described in the parable may be thought of as referring to four kinds of hearts—four different ways of hearing and responding to the God who speaks. All the soil is essentially the same earth. "It's what's happened to it or been added to distort its purpose that delineates the kinds of soil. It's no different with our hearts!"[1] The question is, "What kind of soil is your heart and my heart?" There are at least four possible answers:

Choice A: Hard on the Outside

Jesus observed that some of the seed fell on the trodden path. The soil was hard and impenetrable. The seeds danced on the surface. The birds descended and plucked up a ready meal. The seed and the soil needed each other, but there was no productive contact.

This soil represents the hard-hearted listener—the person who has closed his or her mind and shut off feelings, refusing to discern or hear the will of God. It is like some persons in Jesus' day whose assumptions and prejudices did not allow them even to conceive that Jesus was the Messiah. The Kingdom of God could not penetrate the barriers they had erected.

Or it is like the folks in Jesus' hometown of Nazareth. Jesus "did not do many mighty works there, because of their unbelief" (Matt. 13:58).

Or it is like hard-hearted people who have set ideas and beliefs. Sometimes customs and practices can take on the authority of the Ten Commandments and deafen our ears to what God is saying. A danger is that familiar patterns of life-style and church life become more important than Christ himself. An even greater danger is that we do not live out the convictions that we have—a refusal to live what we already know.

A few years ago, our teenage son had a buildup of wax in his ears. He was amazed at the improvement in his ability to hear after the doctor removed the wax. The wax had collected a little bit at a time until his hearing was almost completely blocked. It is like Christians who have ears but do not hear.

---

1. Lloyd John Ogilvie, *Autobiography of God* (Glendale, CA: GL Regal Books, 1979), p. 54.

Choice B: Hard on the Inside

Jesus observed that some of the seed fell on rocky soil. This does not mean soil that happens to have a few rocks in it. Rather, it refers to bedrock that is covered over with a thin layer of soil. Seeds lodged in this soil take root. Soon, though, the roots reach the impenetrable rock and are not able to grow deeply. Denied depth nourishment, the plant withers in the sun and cannot sustain its initial growth.

This part of the parable describes the listener with a shallow heart. On the surface everything looks good. But lurking underneath is a barrier to continued spiritual growth and development. This may be why so many Christians suffer "burnout." Everything goes well for awhile. Spiritual growth and development seem to be taking place. Then growth seems to stop. Love is not sensed. Joy leaves. Bitterness, anger, depression, or discouragement may appear.

What is the surface layer for me and for you? What forms the rock that resists the root?

Choice C: Conflicting Priorities

Jesus observed that some of the seed fell into ground that was infested by weeds. The soil had within it weed seeds as well as the newly planted good seed. Both would sprout and flourish. But eventually the resources of the soil would be sapped by the weeds. The weeds would crowd out the desired plant.

Many voices clamor for our attention and compete for our loyalties. Worry, riches, and pleasures are mentioned specifically by Jesus. We may get so busy with so many things that we can't hear the voice of God speaking to us. We hear what we are attuned to hear. An illustration I first heard many years ago tells of a young boy from the country who was visiting his cousin in the city. As they were walking on a downtown sidewalk, a man next to them dropped a coin and walked on. The boy from the city heard the coin drop, picked it up, and returned it to the man. He asked his cousin, "Didn't you hear the coin when it struck the sidewalk?" "No," was the reply. A few minutes later, the boy from the country said to his cousin, "Stop! Do you hear that?" "I don't hear anything," said his cousin. "It's a cricket," replied the visitor from the country. We hear what our ears and minds and hearts are attuned to hear.

The gospel of Jesus Christ can be choked out. The good seed of the Kingdom requires that absolute loyalty and first priority be given to God. The good seed does not prosper if it is crowded out by the weeds of our own agendas and prior commitments.

One of the memories of my childhood is hoeing on my grandfather's farm in east Texas when I made my annual visit of two or three weeks during the summer. To hoe cotton does not mean cutting the cotton plants with the hoe. It does mean being able to tell the difference between the cotton and the weeds and then cutting down the weeds that are threatening the growth of the cotton.

We live in a time when there seem to be many "other gods." We need to recognize these idols and identify them as gods with feet of clay that, knowingly or inadvertently, we worship each day. God calls us to examine our loyalties and rearrange our priorities.

What are my thorns? What are yours? What weeding is necessary?

Choice D: Responsive

Jesus observed that some of the seed fell on good soil. It bore fruit and brought forth—some a hundredfold, some sixty, some thirty.

This soil represents the heart that listens and responds. It is a sincere heart. It is a prayerful heart. It bears the fruit of the Spirit. It is open and receptive to the things of God. It is willing to be stirred to the depths. It is willing to give the first priority and allegiance to God.

One of the joys of this parable is that even if much seed is wasted, some seed falls on good soil and a great harvest is sure. This should encourage us when nothing seems to be happening.

As a young man, John Harvard emigrated from England to America. Since he was a brilliant scholar, everyone predicted the brightest future for him. In America he died after only one year. When he died he left a little over £700 and a collection of more than 200 books to a new university in America—a university that became Harvard University. The death of John Harvard looked like waste, but it produced an abundant harvest.

So in your life and in mine, results, though delayed, will come. The harvest is sure.

What answer did you choose in this multiple-choice test? Before you respond, let me mention another possibility:

Choice E: All of the Above

There is some of each type of soil in us, at different times and under varying circumstances. Our hearts are responsive, however, as we move from active listening to God into action.

Action Arenas

Consider the following examples of arenas where the Christian steward might consider taking action:

(1) *Personal witness:* One person speaking to another to present the good news of the gospel of Jesus Christ is a seemingly simple action compared to responses to the two issues mentioned below. Yet, if other persons are expected to respond to such issues, they need to be invited to participate in the journey of the Christian steward. To be a steward is to enlist others to join with you in the steward's journey.

(2) *Justice and peace:* As a boy growing up in Fort Worth, Texas, one of the most solemn occasions was the annual parade on Armistice Day. At the eleventh hour of the eleventh day of

the eleventh month, the parade stopped and there was complete silence for a full minute. People remembered World War I (then known as the Great War) as the war to end all wars. Surely, it was felt, the horrors of World War I were so immense that no nation would ever engage in war again. Tragically this was not to be. As we know all too well, World War II, the Korean War, the Vietnam War, and scores of other wars and conflicts have since afflicted the world.

With the advent of nuclear weapons and intercontinental delivery systems, humankind now has the potential to destroy all human life on the planet.

(3) *Hunger:* For several years a devastating drought crept across the African continent—a drought that left in its wake some 35 million starving men, women, and children. In Ethiopia alone the death toll in one year reached 900,000. Despite prior warnings from numerous relief agencies, the initial response was widespread indifference. The apathy vanished when television footage shot by a BBC crew was aired on NBC in 1984. The scenes showed emaciated children and rows of corpses laid out on the cracked Ethiopian plain. Within hours, contributions began pouring in. The calamity need not have happened. Signs of disaster had been building. But the reports went largely un-read. After 1985 apathy returned and the response diminished. But the cycle was to be repeated again in 1987 and 1988 when the news media again highlighted world hunger. The "on again, off again" response clicked on once more.

As individual Christian stewards, and the church as steward, increasingly witness to others and engage in specific actions, in-viting the poor and dispossessed to share in the distribution of the Lord's righteousness, the role of the church will change sig-nificantly.

Jim Wallis noted that the role of the church is changing al-ready. The church is becoming a new source of resistance to policies that crush the poor and move us closer to nuclear war. Further, the church offers an alternative vision rooted in the bib-lical vision of justice and peace. This new role requires raising basic questions of justice for the world's poor, who are daily robbed by nuclear weapons.[2]

The Journey

What is needed is a mind-set, a life-style, that actively listens to what God is saying—a listening that allows God to plow, blast the bedrock, and weed out the thorns of the soil of your heart. God has made you good soil. God loves you and wants to bring joy to you. God also has something to say to you about this world in which you live. If you are a faithful steward, you will listen, choose, and respond. Not to respond appropriately is to forsake your stewardship. To respond actively and concretely is to be a steward of the purpose and plan of God.

Questions and Suggestions
for Individual Reflection and Action

1. Recall and reflect on a time that you didn't listen to God.

2. Why is it difficult (or not difficult) to listen and respond to God? What are the factors that help and block?

3. What are some specific arenas of action about which you need to listen to and respond to God? What steps can you take to listen and respond better in your life?

4. What are some specific arenas of action about which your congregation needs to listen and respond to God? What steps can you take to be of help?

2. Jim Wallis, *Agenda for Biblical People: A New Edition* (San Francisco: Harper & Row, 1976, 1984), p. xv.

Chapter 4

A Purpose That Attracts

Parable of the Children at Play   (Luke 7:31-35)

"To what then shall I compare the men of this generation, and what are they like? They are like children sitting in the market place and calling to one another,

'We piped to you, and you did not dance;
we wailed, and you did not weep.'

"For John the Baptist has come eating no bread and drinking no wine; and you say, 'He has a demon.' The Son of man has come eating and drinking; and you say, 'Behold, a glutton and a drunkard, a friend of tax collectors and sinners!' Yet wisdom is justified by all her children."

God's Purpose

A key point in being a steward is to have a clear sense of God's purpose. Without purpose there is confusion and despair. With purpose there is direction and hope. Jesus' parable of the children at play (Luke 7:31-35) describes children who cannot agree with one another about what game to play. They argue and complain, with no clear sense of purpose. "We piped to you, and you did not dance. . . ."

*   *   *

"I want to watch television." "I want to play Trivial Pursuit." "We always play what you want. For once, why can't we do what I want?" Who among us has not heard these or similar words and arguments from two or more children? Wouldn't it be great if this style of "dialogue" stopped when human beings mature and leave "childish things" behind?

Unfortunately, we cannot make the assumption that adults escape engaging in such behavior. Even in the church, disputes expressing narrow self-interests can be heard on many occasions. The discussion may center on the use of the church's building by groups from outside the church. Or the order of worship. Or how loudly the organ should be played. Or the amount of the pastor's salary for the coming year. Or how much money the church should give to missions. Or. . . . The list goes on and on. You surely have your own examples.

Within nations, citizens debate purpose. Some argue, "Our first and highest priority is to build the national defense. Unless we are militarily secure, our freedom and liberties cannot be assured." Others contend, "Our first concern must be justice, freedom, and equality for all our people. If these cease to exist, then we are no different from that other nation we fear and criticize so much."

On the world scene, the dialogue among nations is not much improved. "We can't trust the _____s" (Each nation fills in the blank according to its current prejudice.) "If they can kill each of us three times over, then we need to be able to kill them at least six times over." "If we don't have nuclear arms, then they will not be afraid of us, and therefore they won't attack us." Each party feels the other is naive and unrealistic.

God Is Owner

These arguments, dialogues, and discussions have certain things in common: God is ignored, not listened to. In short, God is left out of the equation. An assumption is made that an individual, or a group in the church, or a political party, or a nation can make a decision without recognizing the reality that this earth, indeed this universe, belongs to God by right of creation. Everett S. Reynolds, Sr. expressed this basic truth in words that almost sing aloud:

> God started with nothing and made a world, made this great, grand and glorious world—and everything in it belongs to God alone. Yes, everything in this world belongs to God; it's God's because God made it. The trees, grass, mountains, rivers, men and women, the ability to think, to talk, to walk, to see, to hear, and the ability to transform that which God has given into other things such as material, energy, and food. To work and use the gifts of life, to sing, to draw, to act and to think are all given of God. Yes, the list is endless, all that God has made and allowed us to use and/or transform, comes from our God, who made everything. . . . Our sufficiency is of God.[1]

"The earth is the Lord's and the fulness thereof. . ." (Ps. 24:1). God *is* the Owner.

1. Everett S. Reynolds, Sr., "Our Sufficiency Is of God," in *Thanks*Giving: Stewardship Sermons out of the Ethnic Minority Experience*, ed. J. LaVon Kincaid, Sr. (Nashville: Discipleship Resources, 1984), p. 13.

We Are Stewards

In Genesis 1:27, we read that God created *'adam* "in his image," and this is explained by saying "male and female he created them." The Hebrew word *'adam* is usually translated into English as "man." A more accurate translation of *'adam* is "people" or "humanity." Hebrew has special words for "man" meaning a male human being (*'ish*) and for "woman" (*'ishshah*).

In the New Testament the concept of the "image of God" is used to refer to Jesus Christ. 2 Corinthians 4:4 refers to "the gospel of the glory of Christ, who is the likeness of God." Colossians 1:15 states that Jesus Christ is "the image of the invisible God, the first-born of all creation. . . ."

Those who bear the name of Christ and are baptized and incorporated into the life of Christ are the "image of God," not only by creation, but also by redemption. "You have put off the old nature . . . and have put on the new nature, which is being renewed in knowledge after the image of its creator" (Col. 3:9-10; see also 2 Cor. 3:18; Eph. 4:24; and 1 Cor. 15:49).

When we recall that Jesus Christ is the Chief Steward, we realize that our redemption necessarily involves us as stewards also. Douglas Hall noted that the Christological basis of stewardship means not only that our stewardship is exemplified by Jesus, but that it is the *prior* stewardship of Jesus into which, through the Spirit and faith, we are initiated.[2] This is more than a simple exhortation that Christians ought to be stewards. We participate in the stewardship of Jesus Christ as those who have been brought into identity with him through putting on the new nature. We *are* stewards of God.

---

2. Douglas John Hall, *The Steward: A Biblical Symbol Come of Age* (New York: Friendship Press, 1982), p. 25.

God's Purpose

In the parable recorded in Luke 7:31-35, Jesus compared the "men of this generation" to children arguing in the marketplace about which game they would play. One group wanted to play "weddings," while others wanted to play "funerals." They taunted each other, each group wanting to get its own way. Perhaps neither group really knew what it wanted.

The verse preceding the parable is a key to the interpretation of the parable. "But the Pharisees and the lawyers rejected the purpose of God for themselves. . ." (Luke 7:30). The story of the children at play is Jesus' characterization of those people who rejected the purpose of God. And having rejected the purpose of God, they rejected the messengers of God: John the Baptist because he was too ascetic and Jesus because he ate and drank with tax collectors and sinners. One was too serious; the other was not serious enough. The purpose of God never makes sense unless there is an underlying assumption and understanding that God is the Creator and Owner of the entire universe. Some leaders thought that they "owned" the religious institutions of Israel. They made the rules and regulations. When John the Baptist and Jesus called for repentance and acceptance of the absolute reign and rule of God, saying "the Kingdom of God is at hand," they met strong and determined resistance from these leaders.

We now come to a decisive point about what it means to be a steward of God. To be a steward is:

1. to recognize the reality of God's love (the parable of the prodigal father);
2. to experience the joy that comes when God reaches out in love to a lost world (the parable of the lost sheep);
3. to respond to God (the parable of the soils); and
4. to be led by *God's purpose as Creator and Owner.*

Only as we know and experience the reality of God as Creator and Owner can we know that our ultimate purpose is to love and serve the God who loves us and who owns everything in this universe. Then we are motivated to be the faithful stewards that God wants us to be.

Yet the concept of stewardship is often narrowed to mean simply the means by which the church secures money to fund a spiritual and noble end—the church's "mission." Stewardship is equated with church fund-raising. Others expand stewardship to mean the way in which the individual manages the traditional ingredients of time, talent, and money. These concepts, however, miss the mark of the biblical concept of stewardship.

Servanthood

One essential ingredient often left out is that of servanthood. Jung Young Lee[3] painted a beautiful picture in words of the value of emptiness for Oriental people. In commenting on the reason why bamboo has such special significance for most Asians, he noted that one factor that makes bamboo unusual is that it is hollow. For an Asian, emptiness is often more valuable than fullness.

Lee noted that the Oriental artist usually spends more time and gives more attention to the allocation of empty space than in drawing actual paintings. One of the basic features of an Oriental house is emptiness. If a room is not empty, it is useless. Likewise, the value of a bowl or utensil comes from its emptiness. When the bowl is full, it is of no use.

In Philippians 2:5-11, we read that Christ emptied himself, taking the form of a servant. This passage is one of the finest descriptions of the incarnation of Christ. By emptying himself of the form of God, he was transformed into the form of a servant.

Likewise, we cannot become servants of God unless we empty ourselves of the nature of being a master, of believing somehow that we are the owners and masters. This process of

3. Jung Young Lee, "The Bamboo Tree," in Thanks*Giving: Stewardship out of the Ethnic Minority Experience, ed. Kincaid, p. 8.

emptying ourselves, thereby opening ourselves to a full recognition of God as Owner and Creator, is a significant part of the journey of the Christian steward.

One of the reasons why some Pharisees were critical of others, and why some church members today are critical of others, is that they lack a clear sense of direction based on the purpose of God. People without a clear sense of purpose do not know where they are going. "Be sure of this: if we don't know where we are going, we will be negative and critical of where others want to go."[4]

Failure to see the ministry of the church as participation in God's mission makes it difficult for churches and individuals to participate fully in the purpose of God. Too often gifts by individuals to the church are put into the same category as dues to a club or social organization. Contributions are made out of a sense of obligation, so that the budget can be met. A sense of joy and of participation in God's mission is barely visible, if at all.

Local congregations often place their gifts to the wider mission of the church at the bottom of the priority list. First, it is said, we must maintain the building and pay the salaries. After all, "charity begins at home."

Fulfilling God's Purpose

Life that is lived without a sense of purpose can lead to tragic consequences. A young black man who was engaged in a struggle on the corner of a busy intersection said, "I ain't got nothing to live for. Kill me, I don't care."[5] He didn't know that his life belongs to God—that God is Creator and Owner, that life has no meaning except as men and women and young people find their purpose in God.

4. Lloyd John Ogilvie, *Autobiography of God* (Glendale, CA: GL Regal Books, 1979), p. 133.
5. Reynolds, "Our Sufficiency Is of God," in *Thanks*Giving: Stewardship out of the Ethnic Minority Experience*, ed. Kincaid, p. 14.

Another tragic example is embodied in events in May 1985 in the city of Philadelphia. Members of the radical group MOVE experienced despair, hopelessness, frustration, and rage to such an extent that they declared war on society. The tragic consequences were a bombing and a conflagration that destroyed sixty-one homes and caused the deaths of several people. We live in a world in which despair seems to swallow up hope.

The suffering and pain affecting hundreds of millions of people in famine-stricken Africa and other parts of the world have touched the hearts and purse strings of many people, and rightly so. At the same time it is easy to despair or become cynical when we realize the magnitude of the problem and the politicization of the situation by leaders of some of the affected countries.

The world desperately needs a sense of purpose—a vision. On the night before his assassination in Memphis in 1968, Martin Luther King, Jr. articulated his vision: "I've been to the mountaintop; I've seen the Promised Land. I may not get there with you, but one day, my people will be free."

The strange actions of the prophet Jeremiah illustrate the importance of determining and participating in God's purpose. Do you remember the story? The army of Nebuchadnezzar had laid siege to Jerusalem. At the very time that it was clear that Jerusalem would be destroyed and the Israelites taken as captives to Babylon, Jeremiah purchased land in nearby Anathoth. What kind of time and place was that to make an investment?

Yet it was in such a time of fear and despair that Jeremiah sealed the deed of purchase in an earthen jar and said, "Thus says the LORD of hosts, the God of Israel: Houses and fields and vineyards shall again be bought in this land" (Jer. 32:15). It was the act of a person who trusted in God against all the odds. Jeremiah refused to indulge the fantasy that the exile would soon end. Reality told him otherwise. But he refused to give in to despair. He adopted a life-style of hope.

One of the vital questions that the church of Jesus Christ needs to address is: How can God's word be understood in a time when our accustomed way of life is coming apart? Or, as the psalmist expressed it, "How shall we sing the LORD'S song in a foreign land?" (Ps. 137:4).

God asks us what we really want. Do we really want God's purpose to be carried out in our lives and in the life of the world?

Our Identity

To know that we are Christian stewards is a vital part of participating in the purpose of God. The story of a young lion illustrates this fact.

A young lion got lost one day and his family couldn't find him. After awhile he wandered into a community of lambs and was being brought up by them. They taught the little lion how to baa. It sounded silly to him, but that's what everybody was doing. They taught him how to munch on grass. It tasted lousy, but that's what everybody else was eating. Once in a while he would look down and wonder why he didn't look like everyone else. But, he figured, that's just the way it is.

While he was out munching on grass and baaing one day, there was a huge roar up on the hill. All the little lambs scattered as fast as they could. But somehow in the residue of the mind of the little lion, it sounded familiar. So he went padding off to find out what it was.

When he got there, the big lion looked down and said, "What do you think you're doing?" The little lion said, "I'm munching on grass." "But what are the funny noises you're making?" "I'm baaing."

"Come here," said the big lion. He took the little lion over to a pond of water and said, "Look in the water." The little lion looked in the water and the big lion gave a roar. The little lion's eyes lighted up and he said, "I'm like you." "Right," said the big lion. "Now you know who you are and whose you are."[6]

6. Based on a presentation by John H. Westerhoff III at Syracuse, New York, in May 1982, sponsored by American Baptist Churches of New York State.

In this realization, identity and purpose come together: knowing who we are and whose we are; knowing that we belong to God by right of creation; knowing that God has a purpose. God's purpose will attract us, because it has become *our* purpose.

The Journey

God is with you. You belong to God by creation. Because you are created in the image of God, your identity is inseparably linked to God. Your vocation—your call from God—is to be a faithful steward, determining and carrying out the purpose of God. Your realization of this is a significant step in your journey as a Christian steward. The journey of the Christian steward, informed by God's purpose, leads to a hope-filled life. You are called to choose God's purpose and hope! As the journey continues, God is ready to provide the resources you need to carry out God's purposes.

Questions and Suggestions
for Individual Reflection and Action

1. Do you sometimes leave God out of the equation when thinking about your purpose in life? Why or why not?

2. Are there ways in which you behave as the children in the parable—arguing, with no clear sense of purpose? What are some of those ways?

3. Do you feel yourself to be a Christian steward? What is helping or hindering you at this time?

4. What steps can you take to focus your life on a sense of purpose that puts God into the equation?

PART II

USING RESOURCES AND TAKING RISKS

Having gained a sense of the purpose of God, the steward can experience the reality that God is ready to provide the resources needed to fulfill that purpose. As a steward, you must be willing to accept those resources, use them, and even risk them.

God Is Ready to Provide Resources

Parable of the Neighbor   (Luke 11:1-10)

He was praying in a certain place, and when he ceased, one of his disciples said to him, "Lord, teach us to pray, as John taught his disciples." And he said to them, "When you pray, say:

"'Father, hallowed be thy name. Thy kingdom come. Give us each day our daily bread; and forgive us our sins, for we ourselves forgive every one who is indebted to us; and lead us not into temptation.'"

And he said to them, "Which of you who has a friend will go to him at midnight and say to him, 'Friend, lend me three loaves; for a friend of mine has arrived on a journey, and I have nothing to set before him'; and he will answer from within, 'Do not bother me; the door is now shut, and my children are with me in bed; I cannot get up and give you anything'? I tell you, though he will not get up and give him anything because he is his friend, yet because of his importunity he will rise and give him whatever he needs. And I tell you, Ask, and it will be given you; seek, and you will find; knock, and it will be opened to you. For every one who asks receives, and he who seeks finds, and to him who knocks it will be opened."

Being Aware of God's Readiness to Give You Whatever You Need to Fulfill God's Purpose

God is ready to give you whatever you need to fulfill God's purpose. The parable of the neighbor (Luke 11:1-10) describes the utter availability of God. This abundant generosity of God is a reality that is difficult for most human beings to accept. ". . .he will rise and give him whatever he needs."

*   *   *

An Unexpected Need

Have you ever been awakened out of a sound sleep by a pounding on your front door or the incessant ring of your telephone? You probably have. It is a jarring experience. There is a second or two of disorientation as you try to collect your thoughts and figure out what's going on. Perhaps there is a moment of anger as you wonder why someone would be so rude as to awaken you in the middle of the night. There may be a flash of fear, as you wonder if there is bad news. Perhaps your son or daughter has been in an accident or is in jail. Perhaps a loved one has died. You dread going to the door or picking up the telephone.

Jesus' parable of the neighbor describes such an incident. It is a humorous parable. Jesus often used humor to make his point. Laughter can be an effective preparation for confrontation with the truth.

The typical one-room Palestinian house was divided into two parts: a main floor used by the family during the day and as a stable at night, and a loft at one end where the family ate and slept. When night came, the cattle were brought in and the door bolted with a crossbar. Soon the whole family went to sleep in the loft and the cattle settled down. It was dark and quiet.

Usually it stayed dark and quiet. But not in the parable Jesus told. At midnight, when everyone was sleeping soundly, there came a loud beating on the wooden door. An old friend of the family had come to the village and had no place to stay. Travelers in Palestine often traveled at night to escape the searing heat. The man wondered who was knocking on the door. He got out of bed, stepped carefully over his family, climbed down the ladder, made his way through the cattle, and finally opened the door. Then he greeted his old friend, invited him in, and made a place for him.

But the friend had to be fed, not only because he was hungry, but because it would be unforgivable not to offer a meal. To refuse would make an enemy. But the host had no bread. What to do? His neighbor would help, or would he? There was nothing to do but to try. The host went next door, where his neighbor and his family were also bedded down for the night. The neighbor, however, had small children. We all know how long it takes to get small children to go to sleep. They would be awakened by a midnight knock. But, no matter, the man needed bread for his visitor. He pounded wildly on his neighbor's door. There was no response. He paused, and then knocked again, even more loudly. Finally there was an angry response from inside, "Who's there? What do you want at this hour of the night?"

"Friend, lend me three loaves; for a friend of mine has arrived on a journey, and I have nothing to set before him" (Luke 11:5-6). "In the East hospitality is a sacred duty; and it was not enough to set before a man a bare sufficiency of food."[1] There was a long silence. What would his neighbor say?

The neighbor turned over in bed, determined to go back to sleep. But his children were now awake. "Who was that at the door? What did he say he wanted? Is it morning already?" The cattle began to stir. The whole household was beginning to be disturbed. Again, there was a persistent knocking. "What a neigh-

1. William Barclay, *And Jesus Said: A Handbook on the Parables of Jesus* (Philadelphia: Westminster Press, 1970), p. 113.

bor," he thought. "He will wake up the whole village just to get three loaves of bread." Finally he saw nothing to do but to get up and give him the bread he needed.

Jesus asks us, "Well, what would you have done?" Perhaps we are chuckling as we answer, "Why, we would get up and help the neighbor." Then the conversation takes an unexpected turn. The conversation is serious. If a man would respond because of the persistence of his neighbor, will not God, who neither slumbers nor sleeps (Ps. 121:3), answer our prayers? This is a *"more than that"* method of teaching. How much more God will respond to us. "And I tell you, Ask, and it will be given you; seek, and you will find; knock, and it will be opened to you" (Luke 11:9). God is a gracious, loving Parent. "For every one who asks receives, and he who seeks finds, and to him who knocks it will be opened" (Luke 11:10).

God's Resources

Jesus has told us something significant about how we can communicate with God. God listens to us and responds to us with an availability of resources beyond our wildest expectation. Recall that the eleventh chapter of Luke begins with the disciples asking Jesus how to pray. Jesus responded with "The Disciples' Prayer." Part of the prayer is the petition, "Give us each day our daily bread" (Luke 11:3). God *does* give us what we need, more willingly than the neighbor gave bread in the parable.

Why is it so difficult for most of us to find time to pray? Basically, we find time to do what we want to do. Is it because we think of God as a reluctant neighbor and we don't feel that we can overcome God's reluctance? We want to spend time with a person who loves, accepts, and affirms us. Are we sure about God? Jesus is telling us of the utter availability of God. Just as we sometimes project onto another person some of our inner feelings, so we may be projecting onto God the reluctance that we are feeling. God is ready!

During World War II, citizens of the United States underwent a scarcity of many goods whose ready availability had previously been taken for granted: meat, eggs, sugar, tires, gasoline, and clothing, to name only a few. A system of rationing was established and coupons for various items were issued. As a young teenager, I remember helping in the school auditorium when hundreds of people came in to register in order to receive various types of rationing coupons. Many resources were difficult, or even impossible, to obtain. Most people were willing to endure the hardships "for the duration," as a way of making a contribution to the national effort. Such a wartime experience stands in stark contrast to God's abundant generosity.

Douglas Meeks has stated that the assumption of textbooks on economics is that "scarcity" will always be present. There will never be enough, it is assumed. The gospel radically subverts this assumption. There may be lack or deficiency, but not scarcity. There is *more than enough* if the righteousness of God is at hand.[2]

As we have looked at the journey of the Christian steward, we have seen that it means that we recognize the reality of God's love and experience the joy that God feels in reaching out in love to a lost world. Humans are called to respond to God with full recognition of God as Creator and Owner. We seek to fulfill God's purpose, with a growing sense that God is ready to provide resources far beyond anything we can imagine. God is even more willing to give than we are to receive.

God's Willingness to Share

Why is God willing to share resources with us? Because God has chosen to call us and accept us as servants and stewards. "This is how one should regard us, as servants of Christ and stewards of

2. M. Douglas Meeks in presentations at the Winter Event of the Commission on Stewardship of the National Council of the Churches of Christ in the U.S.A. in December 1985.

the mysteries of God" (1 Cor. 4:1). Perhaps the idea of being a servant is unpleasant or even distasteful to you. Certainly to be the type of servant described in this story from Korea would not appeal to anyone.

Jung Young Lee[3] gave a vivid description of what it means to be a servant. He grew up in Korea in a home that was still wealthy enough to have many servants. As a six-year-old, he had his own servant, a fifteen-year-old boy whom he called Daeji or "Pig." Wherever Jung Young Lee went, his servant had to come along. The servant had to do whatever he was commanded to do.

Lee recalled an incident from his boyhood when he and "Pig" went to a mountain not too far away from their home. There he saw a beautiful flower on the top of a cliff. He pointed at it and asked "Pig" to bring it to him. "Pig" almost lost his life climbing up the cliff. Yet, he had to bring the flower because he was the servant. On another occasion when Lee fell on the playground and hurt himself, he cried loudly as he came into the house. His father was angry at the servant and said, "What were you doing when my son fell down?" "Pig" was beaten up by the father, but could not say a word.

Lee grew up. World War II passed. Then, during the Korean War, he found himself a war refugee traveling to South Korea. Penniless, he had to beg for food to stay alive. Finally, he was taken into a wealthy home where he became the servant of an old man. He described his experiences in these words:

> During the three months of my stay with this man I found out what it means to be a servant. I was the extension of his hands and legs. I had to do exactly and efficiently what my master told me to do. More than that, I had to do what he expected me to do. No matter how much I disagreed with him or how unhappy I was with my work, I could not say a single no to his demands. I was practically his possession. I became his thing, not a person.

3. Jung Young Lee, "The Bamboo Tree," in *Thanks*Giving: Stewardship Sermons out of the Ethnic Minority Experience,* ed. J. LaVon Kincaid, Sr. (Nashville: Discipleship Resources, 1984), p. 9.

I didn't have any rights of my own. My entire existence depended on him. If he had wanted to kill me, he certainly could have. I lived under the shadow of fear and uncertainty.

My master demanded of me absolute obedience, obedience even to death. During those days I recalled my servant "Pig," of my younger days. I came to empathize with those who were oppressed. I learned how inhumane it is to be a servant.[4]

Contrast this with Christ, who "emptied himself," took the form of a servant, and was obedient even to death. His was a voluntary servanthood, done to save the world. We have the privilege of being servants of Christ. It is a voluntary decision; God does not force us.

God's Readiness

In Jesus Christ, God has given us a gift far beyond our wildest imagination. How strange it is, then, when we squander so much of the benefit of that precious gift, failing to realize God's readiness to hear us, to communicate with us. God has given us a great gift.

Harry Emerson Fosdick described God's readiness to give:

> During a dry season in the New Hebrides, John G. Paton the missionary awakened the derision of the natives by digging for water. They said water always came down from heaven, not up through the earth. But Paton revealed a larger truth than they had seen before by discovering to them that heaven could give them water through their own land. So men insist on waiting for God to send them blessing in some supernormal way, when all the while he is giving them abundant supply if they would only learn to retreat into the fertile places of their own spirits where, as Jesus said, the wells of living water seek to rise.[5]

4. Ibid., p. 10.
5. Harry Emerson Fosdick, *The Meaning of Prayer*, quoted by Rueben P. Job and Norman Shawchuck in *A Guide to Prayer for Ministers and Other Servants* (Nashville: Upper Room, 1983), p. 216.

Imagine for a moment that a loved one offered you a gift of something you had longed for. Surely you would rejoice; you would accept the gift; and try to use it wisely. That loved one would have a special place in your heart and affections. You would communicate often. You would express your thanks in many ways.

So it is with God. God has given us a gift beside which all the treasures of this world pale in comparison. We have been given the gift of Jesus Christ. God is not reluctant to be in communication with us as we express our appreciation for this great gift and as we make our needs known. We do not have to pound on the door to gain access to God. God is ready, willing, and able.

Yet, knowing all this—all that God has given to us in Jesus Christ, many Christians feel that their prayers go unanswered, or at least seem to go unanswered. The impact of Jesus' parable is that all prayers are answered. Sometimes, however, God does not answer our prayers in the way or on the schedule we might have preferred. There have been times when I was not ready for the thing for which I was praying. In the painful period of waiting, what I asked for originally was changed. God's apparent silence became God's blessing. I realized that what I had thought was best was not really the best. God's best was greater than I could have imagined. The difficult part is not knowing all this during the waiting period.

As time passed, I learned what is meant by the fullness of time. God's timetable does not always match my timetable. Jesus Christ came to be with us in the fullness of God's time. God "has made known to us in all wisdom and insight the mystery of his will, according to his purpose which he set forth in Christ as a plan for the fulness of time" (Eph. 1:9-10).

The Journey

Jesus made it clear in this parable that God wants to provide resources to you. You don't have to pound on God's door. God is ready. As a matter of fact, God stands outside the door of your heart and my heart, knocking gently and persistently. Yet God does not force his way into your life, but rather waits for you to respond. God is ready to share multiple resources and to give you the great gift. "And my God will supply every need of yours" (Phil. 4:19). Are you ready to accept what God wants to share with you? That is the next step in the journey.

Questions and Suggestions for Individual Reflection and Action

1. What resources is God making available to you at this time? Are there other resources that God wants to make available to you?

2. In what ways is God like or not like the neighbor in the parable? What are your feelings about the "utter availability" of God as expressed in the chapter?

3. Do you as a Christian steward sometimes squander the benefit of God's greatest gift—Jesus the Christ? In what ways?

4. How can you become more aware of the resources that God offers to you?

Chapter 6

Accepting God's Resources

Parable of the Uncompleted Tower   (Luke 14:25-35)

Now great multitudes accompanied him; and he turned and said
to them, "If any one comes to me and does not hate his own
father and mother and wife and children and brothers and sisters, yes, and even his own life, he cannot be my disciple.
Whoever does not bear his own cross and come after me, cannot be my disciple. For which of you, desiring to build a tower,
does not first sit down and count the cost, whether he has enough
to complete it? Otherwise, when he has laid a foundation, and
is not able to finish, all who see it begin to mock him, saying,
'This man began to build, and was not able to finish.' Or what
king, going to encounter another king in war, will not sit down
first and take counsel whether he is able with ten thousand to
meet him who comes against him with twenty thousand? And if
not, while the other is yet a great way off, he sends an embassy
and asks terms of peace. So therefore, whoever of you does not
renounce all that he has cannot be my disciple.

"Salt is good; but if salt has lost its taste, how shall its saltness be restored? It is fit neither for the land nor for the dunghill; men throw it away. He who has ears to hear, let him hear."

Accepting Resources from God

God is ready to give, but you may resist receiving the resources from God that you need to fulfill God's purpose. The parable of the uncompleted tower (Luke 14:25-35), on the surface, tells you that you must make sure you have enough resources before beginning a project. At a deeper level, the parable tells you that, on your own, you will never have enough of what it takes. God's resources are limitless, but you must be willing to accept the resources that God offers to you. "Sit down and count the cost. . . ."

*   *   *

A number of years ago, I was called to serve as pastor of a church in a small village in upstate New York. When my wife and I moved into the parsonage, we were delighted with our new home. However, one thing puzzled us. The house was an older, two-story structure, with a large unfinished basement. At the front end of the house, this dirt basement had a large hole. Surrounding the hole were several large piles of dirt. Naturally we were curious as to why this large hole, surrounded by piles of dirt, was in the basement of the parsonage. When we asked the folk of the church, we learned that the young people of the church, during the pastorate prior to ours, had begun a project of building a youth center in the basement of the parsonage. The project had been started, but was never finished. Perhaps sufficient money was not available; perhaps time and energy ran low. In any event, the project had died, leaving the hole as a monument.

As a matter of fact, the hole and the surrounding piles of dirt remained intact during the seven years that we lived in that parsonage. It was an ongoing reminder of the problems that we may encounter in the allocation of money and resources for well-intentioned projects.

Accepting Resources

In Luke 14, Jesus talked about a man building a tower. "For which of you, desiring to build a tower, does not first sit down and count the cost, whether he has enough to complete it? Otherwise, when he has laid a foundation, and is not able to finish, all who see it begin to mock him, saying, 'This man began to build, and was not able to finish'" (Luke 14:28-30).

Jesus stated the cost of discipleship in terms that cannot be misunderstood. Followers of Jesus must give Jesus Christ and the living God the primary place in their lives, with the result that family and friends, plans, and ambitions are taken up into the relationship with Christ. He introduced the demand of the cross. "Whoever does not bear his own cross and come after me, cannot be my disciple" (Luke 14:27). Count the cost!

Usually the parable of the tower builder is interpreted to mean that we should be sure that we have what it takes to be a disciple of Jesus Christ. The deeper meaning of the parable, for me, is that I, on my own, will never have enough of what it takes.[1]

When God calls us to undertake a task or a mission, it is God who will supply the resources. In and of ourselves, we own nothing. Our calling is to be faithful stewards of what God entrusts to our management, knowing that God's supplies are more than sufficient. Discipleship is not mustering up our own resources so that we can have what is needed, but rather accepting from God whatever is needed in each new situation and relationship.

Salty Stewards

Immediately following the parables of the tower and the kings, Jesus uses "salt" as a metaphor: "Salt is good; but if salt has lost

1. Cf. Lloyd John Ogilvie, *Autobiography of God* (Glendale, CA: GL Regal Books, 1979), p. 161.

its taste, how shall its saltness be restored? It is fit neither for the land nor for the dunghill; men throw it away" (Luke 14:34-35). We are called to be the salt of the earth: tangy Christians. Tang, according to Webster, is a distinguishing characteristic that sets apart or gives a special individuality. There should be a tang about a person who calls himself or herself a Christian steward.

In the ancient world, salt was unobtainable in many parts of the world and was a precious commodity. It was valued both for its taste and for its preservative quality. Evidence of the value of salt is found in the Arab phrase for reaching an agreement, "there is salt between us," and the Persian phrase, "untrue to salt," meaning to be disloyal or ungrateful.

One of the oldest roads in Italy is the Via Salaria—the road of salt. Many of the ancient trade routes related to salt mines and salt pans. In many cultures, cakes of salt were used as money. Soldiers in the Roman army were paid an allowance of salt. This allowance was known as the "salarium," from which we derive the word "salary."

In an age when boredom and lack of purpose and meaning are all around us, the Christian is called to give flavor and zest to life and to help preserve those qualities which grow out of the gospel of Jesus Christ. Because Christians compose a majority of the population in North America, we often fail to realize what it is like to be in the minority, called to be "salt" for a culture.

Anyone who has ever prepared oatmeal knows that salt must be added before the oatmeal is cooked, not afterward. If it is added after cooking, all that you taste is the salt. "In a similar way, Christ can never be added as an afterthought of an already full and committed life."[2] Only as we give Christ first place in our total life—our vision, our plans, our personality, and our priorities—can we invest ourselves in creative giving. Then we can escape the trap of being possessed by our possessions. We only really have what we give away.

2. Ibid., p. 159.

What is true for us individually is also true for us corporately. The gospel is the treasure, the gift of God, committed to the stewardship of the church. The responsibility of the church is to be a living sign and an advocate of this gospel. If we become mired in struggles for institutional survival or "turf protection," we are not being the stewards of the gospel that God has called us to be.

Life-Style Issues

To recognize that God is Owner and that all resources come from God has far-reaching life-style implications. Consider this life-style:

"She never wears a single pair long enough for any of them to need repair." So spoke the narrator on the syndicated television program "Lifestyles of the Rich and Famous," as viewers were given a tour of Cher's 13-bedroom Egyptian-style palace, with a swimming pool guarded by a stone sphinx. The narrator's reference was to Cher's several hundred pairs of shoes. In describing this program, *Newsweek* counseled: "Prepare yourself for shamelessly worshipful celebrations of hedonism, materialism, exhibitionism and voyeurism—in other words, thoroughly irresistible television."[3]

Did you know that, according to the same program, Britain's Princess Diana spends $300,000 a year on clothing, "much of it on hats," or that game show mogul Mark Goodson regularly airmails all of his dirty clothing from his Beverly Hills apartment to a favorite laundress in New York?

One explanation offered by *Newsweek* for this phenomenon is that "The proliferation of opulent prime-time soaps like 'Dallas,' 'Dynasty' and 'Falcon Crest' . . . has created a whole new television audience that longs to live vicariously through the plush existence of the rich."[4]

3. "An Embarrassment of Riches," *Newsweek* 103, no. 14 (April 2, 1984): 74.

4. Ibid., pp. 74-75.

But consider another point of view: "Do not be anxious about your life, what you shall eat or what you shall drink, nor about your body, what you shall put on. Is not life more than food, and the body more than clothing?" (Matt. 6:25).

The Christian steward is called to sense, and to help others to sense, the radical difference between "Lifestyles of the Rich and Famous" and the teachings and life-style of Jesus.

Consider the contrast between events that took place in North America and in Africa in the 1980s.

Farmers in North America were caught in a terrifying economic crunch:

- Farm prices had dropped.
- Markets at home and abroad had dwindled.
- Sources of credit, needed by many farmers, had shrunk.
- Nearly 30 percent of the farmers were sliding toward insolvency.
- Cases of family abuse, alcoholism, and injuries to animals were prevalent.
- Clergy were often required to give assistance in the grief process as a farmstead died.
- Farmers, who had raised food for the world, were forced into bread lines.
- As farms died, towns and cities were affected.

At the same time millions of men, women, and children were experiencing hunger and starvation in Africa:

- An estimated 900,000 men, women, and children died in Ethiopia alone in one year.
- At least 30 African nations were affected by drought.
- More than 150 million people on the African continent were threatened by starvation.
- Whole populations were in danger of extinction.
- In Mozambique, children caught and ate tiny sparrows. Even the birds were emaciated and fewer in number.
- In Ethiopia, doctors performed a gruesome act of triage at

refugee camps, selecting only the hardiest to receive food and clothing. Aid was not wasted on the weak.

* Some small children had to be hand-fed because they had forgotten how to eat.

How do such events, in North America and Africa, relate to one another? How can we speak of dwindling world markets for food at the same time that hundreds of millions of people face starvation? Why were farmers in North America, capable of growing enough food to feed most of the world, forced off the farm?

Can the church of Jesus Christ be "salt" in such circumstances? The answer is "yes," if Christian stewards really believe that God provides the resources needed and are willing to accept those resources. With God, there is no scarcity of resources. There may be lack if we do not accept and distribute the resources. When Jesus fed the multitudes, he said in effect, "My people shall eat." There was enough, with food left over.

As Christian stewards who know that God does make resources available, let us talk and act and live in such a way that apathy does not grip us. Let us not leave unfinished what God calls us to do as Christian stewards.

Freedom to Accept Resources

The church of Jesus Christ must boldly claim the resources God has entrusted to the People of God as faithful stewards. As individuals—men and women, young and old—each of us is called to be a steward of Jesus Christ. If we start by "digging a hole," let's be sure we continue and finish the project.

But how? To accept the resources God offers means a willingness to find freedom and our identity in the power of God. G. K. Chesterton described St. Francis of Assisi as:

> God's tumbler, the court jester who stands on his head for the pleasure of the king. But he also observed that while Francis en-

tertained his lord, he caught a new glimpse of reality himself. With the world upside down, with all the trees and towers hanging head downwards, the visual effect was essentially one of dependence. Instead of taking pride in the strength of Assisi's massive walls, Francis was now amazed to see them suspended by the power of God alone.[5]

The freedom to be human is found not in perfect independence, but in submitting oneself voluntarily to God, the Creator and Owner.

The import of this statement is captured in a story told by Martin Buber:

> Several yeshiva [Jewish seminary] students [were] found by their rabbi one day in the house of study, playing checkers when they should have been studying Talmud. Embarrassed, they returned immediately to their books. But the rabbi smiled and told them not to be ashamed, since they always should study the law wherever they find it. So he asked if they knew the three rules of the game of checkers. Obviously they assumed they knew what they were playing, but none would be so bold as to appear to teach the rabbi. Therefore, the rabbi, the master of the Talmud, Kabbala and Zohar, rehearsed for them the rules of the game of checkers. "First," he said, "one must not make two moves at once. Second, one may move only forward, not backward. And third, when one has reached the last row, then he may move wherever he likes. Such," he said, "is what the Torah teaches." And he left. Only much later did the students grasp what they had been taught that day: that they should not clutter their lives with more than one move at a time, that they should always keep sight of the goal toward which they pressed, and that they would become truly free only as they moved to the last row, making themselves the servants of others. Freedom is discovered in obedience. The secret of playing one's life to its fullest is found in submission to the divine rules of play.[6]

5. Belden C. Lane, "Rabbinical Stories: A Primer on Theological Method," *Christian Century* 98, no. 41 (December 16, 1981): 1308.
6. Ibid.

The Journey

Part of the journey of the Christian steward is a willingness to accept resources from God and to use them freely in obedience to God.

> O God,
> We've wasted
> we've complained
> we've grumbled.
> We've misused our resources
> We've confused
> our needs
> with our wants.
> For these sins
> Father, forgive us.
> Help us
> reset our priorities
> according to Your will.
> Amen.[7]

In the next two chapters, you will be invited to explore some of the particular resources God shares with you.

Questions and Suggestions for Individual Reflection and Action

1. What are the "missing" resources that are needed for you to carry out God's purpose for your life?

2. Why haven't you been willing or able to accept these "missing" resources from God? What do you need to do differently to be able to accept them?

3. Reflect on the same questions in relation to your con-

7. Norma Johnson of Lobatse, Botswana, as quoted by Doris Janzen Longacre in *More-with-Less Cookbook* (Scottdale, PA: Herald Press, 1976), p. 8.

gregation. How can you be of help to your congregation in accepting the resources that God wants the congregation to have?

4. List specific steps for follow-up.

Chapter 7

What Are Your Talents?

Parable of the Talents   (Matthew 25:14-30)

"For it will be as when a man going on a journey called his servants and entrusted to them his property; to one he gave five talents, to another two, to another one, to each according to his ability. Then he went away. He who had received the five talents went at once and traded with them; and he made five talents more. So too, he who had the two talents made two talents more. But he who had received the one talent went and dug in the ground and hid his master's money. Now after a long time the master of those servants came and settled accounts with them. And he who had received the five talents came forward, bringing five talents more, saying, 'Master, you delivered to me five talents; here I have made five talents more.' His master said to him, 'Well done, good and faithful servant; you have been faithful over a little, I will set you over much; enter into the joy of your master.' And he also who had the two talents came forward, saying, 'Master, you delivered to me two talents; here I have made two talents more.' His master said to him, 'Well done, good and faithful servant; you have been faithful over a little, I will set you over much; enter into the joy of your master.' He also who had received the one talent came forward, saying,

'Master, I knew you to be a hard man, reaping where you did not sow, and gathering where you did not winnow; so I was afraid, and I went and hid your talent in the ground. Here you have what is yours.' But his master answered him, 'You wicked and slothful servant! You knew that I reap where I have not sowed, and gather where I have not winnowed? Then you ought to have invested my money with the bankers, and at my coming I should have received what was my own with interest. So take the talent from him, and give it to him who has the ten talents. For to every one who has will more be given, and he will have abundance; but from him who has not, even what he has will be taken away. And cast the worthless servant into the outer darkness; there men will weep and gnash their teeth.'"

Recognizing That Your Time and Talents Are a Trust from God and That You Are Responsible to God for How They Are Used

Among the resources God makes available to you are time and talent. The parable of the talents (Matt. 25:24-30) makes it clear that your talent is whatever God has entrusted to you. That which you call "your time" and "your talent" are really entrusted to you by God. You are responsible to God for their use. "A man going on a journey called his servants and entrusted to them his property. . . ."

*　　　*　　　*

Have you heard people excuse themselves by appealing to what they do *not* have? "I'm too old." "I'm too young." "I'm not educated." "I'm too busy." "I'm not good enough." "I could never do that."

When God asked Moses to tell Pharaoh to let the children of Israel go, Moses used a number of phrases to complain about what he did not have: "Who am I that I should go. . . ?" "I am not eloquent. . . ." "Behold, they will not believe me. . . ." (See Exodus 3 and 4.)

After listening to Moses' complaints, God said to him: "What is that in your hand?" In effect God said, "Moses, I am not interested in what you do not have; I am only interested in what you do have. . . . Stretch forth your hand . . . and certainly I will be with you."

Talents Discovered

One of the great fulfillments in pastoral ministry is to see previously unrealized talents of members of the congregation surface and become actively used. One congregation I served had as a member a middle-aged woman who had served the church for many years in "behind the scenes" ministries: working in the kitchen, cleaning classrooms, making favors for a dinner, and doing many other tasks. The thought of standing in front of the congregation, or even a small group, terrified her. She wanted someone else to take the "up front" leadership responsibilities.

As her pastor, I saw a potential in her that she had not seen in herself. Others in the church also sensed this potential hiding beneath the surface. Over a period of time, several members of the congregation and I strove to increase her self-confidence and to encourage her to accept some relatively minor, short-term responsibilities in the church's leadership. At first she was very hesitant and protested that she couldn't do it. Gradually she accepted certain leadership tasks and carried them out beautifully. We offered her encouragement, support, and specific help and training. Her confidence increased and she moved more actively into visible church leadership. Successively she served as a church school teacher, church school superintendent, chair of the Christian education committee, and president of the women's organization. She still enjoyed doing many of the "behind the scenes" ministries, but she had come to realize that God had entrusted other talents to her as well. Those talents were not buried!

Another member of a congregation I served was a woman in her twenties, married with a son and a daughter. Many of us could sense tremendous abilities and depth of spirit in her, even though she did not have a high level of confidence in herself. With encouragement she grew in self-confidence and willingness to accept leadership responsibilities—minor at first, and then very significant. Over the next several years she became one of the most capable and respected leaders in the church.

The day came when she told me that she felt God calling her into pastoral ministry. I rejoiced with her. This meant resuming her college education on a part-time basis. Then, on the completion of college, she entered seminary. Today she has completed her theological education, has worked part time for her denomination on the regional level, and recently began full-time pastoral ministry.

Talents Entrusted

The parable of the talents tells us that God creates and that God calls us to be co-creators in the unfolding of history. To help that become reality, God invests in us and expects a return on that investment.

The parable was based on a common custom in Jesus' day: owners of great properties and estates often traveled for long periods of time on business. While away, they entrusted their responsibilities to servants, usually referred to as stewards. As a matter of fact, several of Jesus' parables focus on persons who go away, leaving their investments, vineyards, or kingdom in the care of trusted servants.

In the parable of the talents, a man set out on a journey, entrusting his property to his servants. It is important that we recognize from the outset that this man represents God. It is God who owns the world. The disciples are the servants.

Three of the servants were singled out. One was given five talents, another two talents, and still another one talent. A talent was originally a measure of weight. Later the term came to designate a fixed sum of silver or gold. While it is difficult to place a monetary value on the talent, it has been estimated that the value of a talent in U.S. currency in the 1980s was approximately $10,000.

Putting the parable in that coinage tells us that one servant received $50,000, one $20,000, and the third $10,000. Quite a trust! Each servant had much to work with while the owner was gone. Each was expected to invest and multiply what had been entrusted to him. What would you do if you were given something of great value and asked to take responsibility for its use?

The first two servants traded, probably taking some risks, and doubled the money entrusted to them. One man then had $100,000, and the other $40,000.

The one-talent man was of a different stripe. He was fearful and therefore cautious. There was no risk taking for him. He hid the talent in the earth. It was buried. The possibility of failure loomed so fiercely in his mind that he could not bring himself to put the talent to any use.

Accountability for Talents

The owner returned and called for an accounting. The first two servants returned to him the results of their work—$140,000 from their adventuresome trading. Notice that the money never belonged to the servants. The whole amount was returned to the owner. And to each of them he said, "Well done, good and faithful servant; you have been faithful over a little, I will set you over much; enter into the joy of your master" (Matt. 25:21).

The one-talent man hung back. He was not so eager. He had heard the praise given to the first two and his defensive mechanism began to put together an explanation as to why he had buried the talent entrusted to him. And what did he do but put the blame on the owner. "Master, I knew you to be a hard man, reaping where you did not sow, and gathering where you did not winnow; so I was afraid, and I went and hid your talent in the ground. Here you have what is yours" (Matt. 25:24-25).

The response of the owner was severe: "You wicked and slothful servant! You knew I reap where I have not sowed, and gather where I have not winnowed? Then you ought to have invested my money with the bankers, and at my coming I should have received what was my own with interest. So take the talent from him, and give it to him who has the ten talents" (Matt. 25:26-28). The third servant had completely miscalculated the owner. He had projected his own fear and insecurity onto the master.

William Barclay noted a tendency in much of religion to avoid the risk of penetrating more deeply into the truth of God, much as the third servant in the parable.

> It is so easy to worship the past, to look back on what we believe to have been a golden age instead of forward to the greater things which shall be. Bishop Lesslie Newbigin of the South India

Church tells how, when plans for the United Church in South India were being discussed, one of the things that kept holding matters up was the demand to know where this course of action was leading. When this had gone on for some time, someone rose and said, "The demand to know where we are going is one which no Christian has a right to make." The Christian must follow truth as blind men long for light, wherever the truth may lead.[1]

The word "talent" has come into our language from this parable. Rather than money, however, it has come to mean abilities and special gifts.

We must be careful, however, not to interpret the parable of the talents simply on the basis of the meaning of the word "talent" that has evolved over the years. Rather, the crucial question that each person must ask is, "What did Jesus mean by the talent?" I would submit that *everything you have and everything you are comprise the talents entrusted to you by God.* This includes your abilities; each precious moment of every day, every week, every month, and every year given to you; your material and financial resources; your relationships with loved ones and friends; the gift of God's salvation and redemption in Jesus Christ—in short, your very life! All of this is entrusted to you by God. And you are called to be God's steward.

What an adventure this makes of life! Yet how often we are like the one-talent man. Our faith, instead of being an adventure, becomes a heavy chain of obligations. We cling to the status quo, hoping we can get by without too many crises or challenges. We are content with the usual routine in the life of the church. The one-talent Christian fails to see how much he or she is needed. The result is a deadly lethargy.

The one-talent person has been compared to a note on a piano. The failure of one note can wreak havoc if that note is silent or sour.

In actuality, no woman or man is one-talented. We are all

1. William Barclay, *And Jesus Said: A Handbook on the Parables of Jesus* (Philadelphia: Westminster Press, 1970), p. 170.

many-talented. We can speak, vote, work, and pray. We can smile. God calls us to realize the potential of our lives, to maximize the years of our lives. This is exciting. God has given to each one of us an urgent purpose. And this purpose demands the very best that we can believe and can give.

The parable makes it very clear that, as stewards, we are accountable to God. With accountability there are consequences. Jesus' point was that talents are entrusted to us to be used. If an opportunity is not taken, it is lost. An arm not used will atrophy. The Christian steward is called to live in courageous faith.

The front page of a Texas newspaper a few years ago carried the

> picture of a young and beautiful Black mother born without arms and legs. The State Department of Public Welfare had charged in court that she was incapable of taking care of the five-month-old daughter.
>
> During the court hearing the mother surprised everyone by proving she was competent to take care of her baby. There before their eyes she undressed and then dressed the baby again by using only her lips and tongue. The judge was so impressed that he not only awarded custody of the baby to her, but said, "I have to commend you very much for your courage, spirit, and ingenuity. . . . You have proven that physical endowments are only a part of the spectrum of resources that human beings possess. . . ."[2]

The young mother was a good steward of her wounds. She did not dwell on what she did not have. Rather, she chose to use to the utmost what God had given to her.

Obviously, we cannot use our talents if we are not willing to invest the time that developing and using skills and abilities requires. God gives each of us 24 hours every day.

---

2. Zan Holmes, Jr., "The Stewardship of Life's Leftovers," in *Thanks*Giving: Stewardship Sermons out of the Ethnic Minority Experience*, ed. J. LaVon Kincaid, Sr. (Nashville: Discipleship Resources, 1984), p. 44.

The Journey

The challenge is to ask yourself how you can use your resources of time and talent for God. What is that special thing which you can do that nobody else in the world can do in quite the same way? Is it to laugh, to smile? Is it an ability to encourage and inspire? Is it an ability to pray? Is it a loving tone people hear in your voice? Is it skill in music or art or teaching or managing or. . . ? The possibilities are almost limitless. What are those things the Owner of all things has entrusted to you? How have you responded to that trust? How are you doing as a steward of Jesus Christ? The next chapter will focus on the money entrusted to you.

Questions and Suggestions
for Individual Reflection and Action

1. Identify the talents that God has entrusted to you. Prayerfully and thoughtfully make a list, being as honest as possible. Then consult with two or three trusted friends or family members who know you well. If it seems appropriate, revise your list, taking into account their comments and suggestions.

2. Since God has entrusted a unique set of talents, skills, and abilities to each person, consider what specific avenues of service God may wish you to follow. Make a list of possibilities. Again, consult with a few trusted friends or family members for affirmation or possible alternative suggestions. Continue to be in prayer as you consider and reconsider possibilities.

3. Ask yourself, "In light of the parable, how am I as a Christian steward held accountable for the use of the talents, abilities, and skills that God has entrusted to me?"

4. If you have not already done so, begin to formulate a specific plan that will include God's use of your talents and abili-

ties. Take into account your ongoing journey on the "stepping stones of the steward" as your plan is developed and implemented.

Chapter 8

Your Money or Your Life!

Parable of the Rich Fool   (Luke 12:13-21)

One of the multitude said to him, "Teacher, bid my brother divide the inheritance with me." But he said to him, "Man, who made me a judge or divider over you?" And he said to them, "Take heed, and beware of all covetousness; for a man's life does not consist in the abundance of his possessions." And he told them a parable, saying, "The land of a rich man brought forth plentifully; and he thought to himself, 'What shall I do, for I have nowhere to store my crops?' And he said, 'I will do this: I will pull down my barns, and build larger ones; and there I will store all my grain and my goods. And I will say to my soul, Soul, you have ample goods laid up for many years; take your ease, eat, drink, be merry.' But God said to him, 'Fool! This night your soul is required of you; and the things you have prepared, whose will they be?' So is he who lays up treasure for himself, and is not rich toward God."

Viewing Money as a Means of Serving God and Helping Others

Another resource God entrusts to you is money. The parable of the rich fool (Luke 12:13-21) states clearly the danger of self-delusion if you regard the use of that money as yours rather than God's. "Soul, you have ample goods laid up for many years; take your ease, eat, drink, be merry."

*   *   *

Jack Benny played variations of a particular sketch numerous times on radio and television. Benny, of course, was well known for his stinginess in these portrayals. He hated to part with even a nickel. (In real life he was quite generous.) The sketch went something like this. A robber would come up to Benny, point a gun at him, and say, "Your money or your life!" A long pause would ensue as Benny hesitated. Again the robber would say, "You heard me. Your money or your life!" Again, a pause, and then Jack Benny, with exquisite timing, would say, "I'm thinking; I'm thinking." Inevitably, there was loud laughter from the studio audience.

We smile briefly as we hear the story now. It seems incongruous to us that a person would seriously consider choosing to die for the sake of the money he or she was carrying in a billfold or purse. Or is it? It is not difficult to lose one's moorings and sense of direction in life. Money can have a mighty grip.

Becoming Rich

In the story that we usually refer to as the parable of the rich fool, Jesus told of a rich man whose productive farm yielded fine crops. His barns were full to overflowing.

> ". . . and he thought to himself, 'What shall I do, for I have nowhere to store my crops?' And he said, 'I will do this: I will pull down my barns, and build larger ones; and there I will store

all my grain and my goods. And I will say to my soul, Soul, you have ample goods laid up for many years; take your ease, eat, drink, be merry.'" (Luke 12:17-19)

Was this success? Many would say so. Isn't that what we dream about? Make all you can as fast as you can. Then retire, sit back, and take life easy. He had accomplished what he had set out to do. What more could a person ask for? But he had missed the purpose of his life.

The story did not end as the man had expected it would. We read, "But God said to him, 'Fool! This night your soul is required of you; and the things you have prepared, whose will they be?' So is he who lays up treasure for himself, and is not rich toward God" (Luke 12:20-21).

In the parable, the rich man used the pronoun "I" six times; "my" is used five times; and even a "you" is used to refer to himself. His whole life was turned in upon himself. His inner conversation was with himself, not with God.

Spending all his time and energy on himself made him equivalent to an oil refinery that does not need any marketing or sales department nor any barrels or pipeline to ship its product because it consumes all of the oil it refines.[1]

William Barclay recounted an old story about

> three apprentice devils who were coming from hell to earth to serve their time. They were telling Satan before they left what they proposed to do. One said, "I will tell men that there is no God." "That," said Satan, "will not do because in their heart of hearts they know there is." "I will tell men," said the second, "that there is no hell." "That," said Satan, "is still more hopeless for even in life they have experienced the remorse of hell." "I will tell men," said the third, "that there is no hurry." "Go," said Satan, "tell them that and you will ruin them by the million."[2]

1. Cf. William F. Keucher, *An Exodus for the Church: From Yesterday to Tomorrow* (Valley Forge, PA: Judson Press, 1973), p. 68, where the illustration of the oil refinery is used to describe the institutional church.

2. William Barclay, *And Jesus Said: A Handbook on the Parables of Jesus* (Philadelphia: Westminster Press, 1970), pp. 124-25.

The "rich fool" and many others forget that the days of each human life are finite and that time does run out.

Some Assumptions to Be Checked

Lest we deceive ourselves, it is appropriate to remember that, in contrast with hundreds of millions of people in this world, most of us who live in North America have more than enough of life's necessities. This affluence has generated a sort of "no-limits" mentality[3] which has assumed that "the sky's the limit." If a woman, or a man, really wants to succeed, success is inevitable. If a person does not pull himself or herself up by the bootstraps, we know whose fault that is!

We often make certain assumptions about ourselves and the world in which we live:

- Nature has a virtually infinite storehouse of resources available for human use.
- Humanity has the right to control nature.
- The best way to attain individual betterment is to improve one's standard of living.
- Economic growth is always good.
- Human powers can make history turn out right.
- Human failures can be overcome by effective problem solving which will be effective if reason and good will are present and science and technology imaginatively developed and applied.
- The successful person is the achiever.
- Persons who are diligent, hardworking, and educated will attain their goals.
- Material abundance brings freedom of choice and a greater happiness.[4]

3. Bruce C. Birch and Larry L. Rasmussen, *The Predicament of the Prosperous* (Philadelphia: Westminster Press, 1978), p. 21.
4. Adapted from a list of assumptions in ibid., pp. 44-45.

Such assumptions, however, ignore basic realities in our world today. Increasingly, as Christian stewards, we see the fallacy behind such assumptions: namely, that the human race owns the resources of this earth and, therefore, is in charge. God the Owner, who has entrusted money and other resources to us, is in charge. We are accountable to God for the way we use these resources to help our brothers and sisters in need. In short, whose household is it? It is God's household, and we are called to live in obedience to the rules of God's household.

The Bible's assumption is that money and possessions are spiritual concerns and reveal more about an individual than any other aspect of life. Consider these words from the New Testament:

> "But woe to you that are rich, for you have received your consolation. Woe to you that are full now, for you shall hunger." (Luke 6:24-25)

> "It is easier for a camel to go through the eye of a needle than for a rich man to enter the kingdom of God." (Matt. 19:24)

> "Whoever of you does not renounce all that he has cannot be my disciple." (Luke 14:33)

> "Do not lay up for yourselves treasures on earth, where moth and rust consume and where thieves break in and steal, but lay up for yourselves treasures in heaven, where neither moth nor rust consumes and where thieves do not break in and steal. For where your treasure is, there will your heart be also." (Matt. 6:19-21)

> "'Lord, when did we see thee hungry or thirsty or a stranger or naked or sick or in prison, and did not minister to thee?' Then he will answer them, 'Truly, I say to you, as you did it not to one of the least of these, you did it not to me.'" (Matt. 25:44-45)

> "Take heed, and beware of all covetousness; for a man's life does not consist in the abundance of his possessions." (Luke 12:15)

Changing a Life-Style

Christians and others around the world have been touched by the plight of the starving men, women, and children in Ethiopia and other parts of Africa, as well as on other continents. Churches in North America and elsewhere have responded significantly through special offerings. But our responsibility as Christian stewards goes far beyond taking such offerings.

The issue is one of life-style. Charles Birch stated, "The rich must live more simply that the poor may simply live."[5] Kenneth Boulding put it this way, "The only way to make the poor richer is to make the rich poorer."[6] These are hard words for most of us. Unless we happen to number ourselves with those who are among the world's truly poor, it is difficult for us to imagine the conditions in which many people live. Robert Heilbroner drew this picture:

> We begin by invading the house of our imaginary American family to strip it of its furniture. Everything goes: beds, chairs, tables, television sets, lamps. We will leave the family with a few old blankets, a kitchen table, a wooden chair. Along with the bureaus go the clothes. Each member of the family may keep in his "wardrobe" his oldest suit or dress, a shirt or blouse. We will permit a pair of shoes for the head of the family, but none for the wife or children.
>
> We move to the kitchen. The appliances have already been taken out, so we turn to the cupboards. . . . The box of matches may stay, a small bag of flour, some sugar and salt. A few moldy potatoes, already in the garbage can, must be hastily rescued, for they will provide much of tonight's meal. We will leave a handful of onions, and a dish of dried beans. All the rest we take away:

5. Charles Birch, "Creation, Technology and Human Survival: Called to Replenish the Earth," *Ecumenical Review* 27, no. 1 (January 1976): 70, as quoted by Birch and Rasmussen, ibid., p. 33.

6. Kenneth Boulding, *Anticipation*, no. 7 (1971), p. 15, as quoted by Birch and Rasmussen, ibid.

the meat, the fresh vegetables, the canned goods, the crackers, the candy.

Now we have stripped the house: the bathroom has been dismantled, the running water shut off, the electric wires taken out. Next we move away from the house. The family can move to the woodshed. . . .

Communications must go next. No newspapers, magazines, books—not that they are missed, since we must take away our family's literacy as well. Instead in our shantytown we will allow one radio. . . .

Now government services must go. No more postman, no more firemen. There is a school, but it is three miles away and consists of two classrooms. . . . There are, of course, no hospitals or doctors nearby. The nearest clinic is ten miles away and is tended by a midwife. It can be reached by bicycle, provided that the family has a bicycle, which is unlikely. . . .

Finally, money. We will allow our family a cash hoard of five dollars. This will prevent our breadwinner from experiencing the tragedy of an Iranian peasant who went blind because he could not raise the $3.94 which he mistakenly thought he needed to receive admission to a hospital where he could have been cured.[7]

Questions begin to come to us: Can we simplify our life-style, or will we do all we can to stay where we are? As Christian stewards, are we willing to let changes take place in our lives?

How Much Is Enough?

The occasion when Jesus observed a widow placing two mites in the temple treasury is pertinent. We know the story well. The point, of course, is that she gave all she had. Jesus commented that she had given more than all the others put together.

7. Robert L. Heilbroner, *The Great Ascent: The Struggle for Economic Development in Our Time,* pp. 33-36, as quoted by Birch and Rasmussen, ibid., pp. 39-40. This vivid description has appeared in various forms over the past 20 years or so. The original source is not known to me.

The point Jesus made is that the amount we give is not important, in and of itself. "The gift that counts is the gift that costs. Or conversely, the gift that costs is the gift that counts."[8]

The rich fool in Jesus' parable thought he had many great possessions. Actually, his possessions possessed him. He laid up treasure for himself, but he was not rich toward God. God wants us to have more than the abundance of things. Jesus lived, died, and rose again to offer us the gift of abundant life.

Richness toward God develops as we allow God to use us in areas of responsibility. When we can honestly say, "Lord, there is nothing I have achieved without your grace," we are beginning to experience richness toward God.

> A story is told of a man who went each day to his backyard and uncovered his money which was buried in the ground. He would then put it back in the ground and cover it up again. To his shock and disappointment, on a particular day, he dug up the ground only to discover that his money was gone! He began to cry out in dismay. His neighbor heard his cry and came to his aid right away. Upon discovering his plight, the neighbor dropped his head, walked away, and said, "What's all the fuss about, you were not using the money for any good anyway! Maybe whoever got it will use it for some good."[9]

Stewardship is about a great deal more than money. As we have already noted, it is about the use of the time and talents God has given us, and much more. It is about the way we value and treasure the gospel of Jesus Christ. But it *is* about money.

My vision is of a Christian community that knows "enough is enough." It would be a community that would remember the ancient words of Proverbs:

8. Joseph B. Bethea, "Costly Giving," in *Thanks*Giving: Stewardship Sermons out of the Ethnic Minority Experience*, ed. J. LaVon Kincaid, Sr. (Nashville: Discipleship Resources, 1984), p. 59.

9. J. LaVon Kincaid, Sr., "Is God in Your Budget?," in *Thanks*Giving*, ed. J. LaVon Kincaid, Sr., p. 71.

Remove far from me falsehood and lying;
give me neither poverty nor riches;
feed me with the food that is needful for me,
lest I be full and deny thee, and say,
"Who is thy Lord?" (Prov. 30:8-9)

Such a community would have people who would be willing to take risks in order to reach out toward great hopes and plans, toward a future they might never see. It may not be practical. It would seem practical to build bigger barns! But we have already heard God's judgment on that philosophy.

Reaching out in risk may be like the people who plant date palms instead of pumpkins, even though they could eat pumpkins in six months, but will not live long enough to harvest dates. Pumpkins, no doubt, will be planted in abundance in our world. Dates will not.[10] "In the grand tradition of Jeremiah, the church . . . can and ought to be among those who plant dates."[11]

In the twelfth chapter of Luke, Jesus went on to say, "Therefore I tell you, do not be anxious about your life, what you shall eat, nor about your body, what you shall put on. For life is more than food, and the body more than clothing" (Luke 12:22-23).

The Journey

The challenge comes to you, as it did to Jack Benny, "Your money or your life." Have you chosen life—an abundant life with God? The next chapter will explore God's call to risk *all* the resources God has entrusted to you in your journey.

10. Alves, *Tomorrow's Child*, as cited by Birch and Rasmussen in *The Predicament of the Prosperous*, p. 191.
11. Ibid., pp. 191-92.

Questions and Suggestions
for Individual Reflection and Action

1. In light of the parable and if God is owner of "your" money, what does that say about your life-style and how you make financial decisions?

2. Examine your checkbook and other financial records. It has been said that a person's checkbook is a theological statement. Write for yourself what you learned as you reflected on your financial records.

3. Prayerfully consider if there are changes in life-style and financial matters that you wish to make. Consider how you can better increase your financial support of God's mission through your congregation.

4. Continue to develop your plan as a Christian steward, taking into account life-style and financial considerations.

Chapter 9

Risk Taking

Parables of the Treasure and the Pearls
(Matthew 13:44-45)

"The kingdom of heaven is like treasure hidden in a field, which a man found and covered up; then in his joy he goes and sells all that he has and buys that field.

"Again, the kingdom of heaven is like a merchant in search of fine pearls, who, on finding one pearl of great value, went and sold all that he had and bought it."

Being Willing to Take Risks

If you are to carry out God's purpose as a Christian steward, it is necessary to take risks in using the resources entrusted to you. The parables of the treasure and the pearls (Matt. 13:44-45) tell you that you are called to give everything to possess the treasure of the kingdom. "A man . . . goes and sells all that he has and buys that field."

*   *   *

One of the vivid memories I have from my childhood when I lived in Fort Worth, Texas, is the annual summer visit I made to my grandparents who scratched out a living on a dirt farm in Lone Oak. The livestock consisted of two or three dairy cows, a horse, two mules, and fifteen or twenty chickens, some of which laid an egg occasionally. The land was used to plant a vegetable garden for the family's use, to grow some hay and corn for the livestock, and to raise cotton as a cash crop.

When I was about ten years old, my grandfather let me operate the plow for a few minutes. It was not a large, modern, mechanized plow; it was a single-blade plow. Nor was it operated by an engine. The power came from Red, one of the two mules. Texas can be very hot in the summertime. And it was hot that day—probably 100 degrees in the shade, and there was no shade. I thought it would be easy work—after all, Red was supplying the muscle power. But I soon discovered that it wasn't all that easy. The plow kept hitting rocks and hard clods of dirt that knocked it off its course, and the mule kept right on pulling. It was not easy to plow a straight furrow. Steering the plow seemed to defy logic. If I tipped the plow to the left, it did not steer to the left but to the right. Soon the sweat was pouring off me. I was hot, tired, and confused. What I had thought would be a relatively easy job turned out to be very difficult. I finished four rows and turned the plow back over to my grandfather.

Risking Everything

I can empathize with the plowman Jesus described in the parable of the buried treasure. He was working in someone else's field. Probably it was very hot and the sweat was pouring off his brow. Possibly slivers from the plow handle were working their way into his hands. The work was monotonous. Suddenly the plow hit an obstruction. There is a legend which says that when the earth was created, God sent an angel with two bags of rocks to spread around the whole earth. One of the bags broke over Palestine and it got half the world's supply.[1] The plowman probably thought, "Another rock to be dug up and carried over to the edge of the field." He stopped the plow. (At least he could stop his plow more easily than I had been able to.) He began to dig in the earth with his hands. But he did not find a rock. Instead, it was a buried chest.

His heart began to beat faster. Could it be? He knew that people often buried their treasure in the earth at times of war or disaster, hoping to return to claim them in the future. "The Rabbis . . . had a proverbial saying, 'There is only one safe repository for money—the earth.'"[2] He opened the chest and found that it was filled with a great treasure—gold, silver, coins, jewelry. He looked around quickly to see if anyone was watching. Then he dug the hole deeper and reburied the chest. As calmly as possible, he finished the day's work and then rushed home to his wife.

"Give me everything that we can possibly sell, everything! We'll even sell the house if we have to!" He explained what had happened. The next day he sold everything he owned, took the money it brought, and negotiated with the owner of the land to buy the land. The land was his—and the treasure along with it. He was gripped by joy. He had given up everything he possessed,

1. LaRue A. Loughhead, *Sayings and Doings of Jesus: His Parables and Miracles Firsthand* (Valley Forge, PA: Judson Press, 1981), p. 18.
2. William Barclay, *And Jesus Said: A Handbook on the Parables of Jesus* (Philadelphia: Westminster Press, 1970), p. 67.

but what he had obtained was worth far more. His mind was not on what he had given up, but on the treasure he had found. He "seized the crucial moment when it came."[3]

Setting Priorities

Willingness to take risks assumes a prior process of establishing priorities. Until priorities are set, there will be no reason to engage in risky actions. LaRue Loughhead described a values-clarification exercise for youth in which he displayed objects such as a stereo album, a candy bar, blue jeans, a red heart, a dollar bill, a school textbook, a picture of a home, a Bible, and a few other things. He asked the students to make a list and rank the objects by order of priority in their lives. He reported:

> The Bible made it to the top of one or two lists. However, I suspect it was there not because the Bible (and what it represents) really was top priority in the lives of those young people but because they thought that that was what I would want them to do, or because that's where they thought they ought to put it on a list made out in church.[4]

Adults go through a similar kind of values-clarification exercise every day, but it's not a game. The setting of priorities does not come without struggle and even pain.

> Spread out before us are all the things we might value: a better house, a new car, a college diploma, a color television, the Bible, a cabin in the mountains, membership in a country club, or a pocket calculator. There they are: all spread out before us. What's the top priority on our lists right now? What's our pearl of great price—the treasure for which we would give almost any-thing—the something of surpassing worth?[5]

3. Ibid., p. 71.
4. Loughhead, *Sayings and Doings of Jesus*, p. 19.
5. Ibid.

What (or Who) Is the Treasure?

To put it another way, "What is it that means that much to us? So much that we would joyfully risk everything we own to gain it?" Does God mean that much to us? Does the gospel of Jesus Christ rate as our highest priority? Would we give up all for the sake of the Kingdom of God? These are questions that, if we take them seriously, fairly take our breath away.

But the meaning of the parable probes to an even deeper level. Recall that God is the leading character in most of the parables Jesus told. Think of God as the plowman in this parable. Then a new truth bursts forth from the parable. What is the treasure sought by God so ardently, so passionately, with such intensity of purpose, that God gave the greatest gift possible to obtain it? Then it hits us. Jesus is saying that we—you and I—are the treasure sought by God. The death of Jesus—the suffering and pain of Calvary—is the price God paid for you and me.[6]

Then we remember the twin parable told by Jesus—the parable of the pearl—that describes the search by the merchant for the one pearl of great price. When the merchant found that pearl, he sold all that he had and purchased it. Pearls, of course, result from invasion and injury of the oyster.

> A grain of sand gets within the oyster and injures it. The oyster then covers over the injury with macle and mother-of-pearl, layer on layer, until the pearl is fashioned. The wounding is the source of the wonder.[7]

The Kingdom of God could not be fulfilled without the terrible wounding of Calvary.

The metaphors of the parables then cut in two ways: what Christ means to us and what we mean to Christ! Too often we picture God as coming to take something from us, when the reality is that God comes to give something to us.

6. Adapted from Lloyd John Ogilvie, *Autobiography of God* (Glendale, CA: GL Regal Books, 1979), p. 111.

7. Ibid., p. 112.

Fear of Risking

There is a story of a preacher who, hearing about the plight of one of his parishioners, collected money to pay her past-due rent. With the money in hand, he knocked on her door. There was no answer. He knocked again and again, still without response. He sensed that she was there, but she did not come to the door. He turned away with the gift undelivered. Later the woman confessed to him that she had heard the knocking, but thought that the landlord had come for the rent. She was not willing to risk opening the door, and thus she missed out on receiving the gift. God has a gift for us—a gift purchased at a great price. Are we willing to take the risk to receive it?

When the reality of what God has done for you and me sinks in, we are motivated to respond to God. We can "seek first the Kingdom of God" only after we have known and experienced the reality that God loved us, sought us out, and bought us at a great price. Then it is love responding to love.

Churches also are called to take risks. Charlie W. Shedd described a risk-taking church business meeting in which the charter members voted to be a dollar-for-dollar mission church. This would mean that for every dollar they spent on the local program, a matching dollar would be sent elsewhere. As a consequence, purchase of any item meant double payments, whether a pencil, paper, or stencils.

But that was not the end of the story. In their denomination, such a dollar-for-dollar commitment did not include building funds. Capital improvements need not be matched. When the people gathered to vote on whether to build a million-dollar sanctuary, they heard a challenge from a young officer, new on the church board. No one there, including the pastor, was expecting strong leadership from him. He stood to sound this call: "When I was elected, the church treasurer told me, 'Man, don't ever forget there's one reason this church gets money. That's because it's giving so much.' I'm on the committee to raise this million dollars. If we vote to build our sanctuary, here's my proposition: I move we go after two million, and give the extra million to build new churches where they're needed. Like on the mission field. Or places in our own country where they could use a hand from us."

Heated discussion followed. When the ballots were counted, 93 percent had affirmed the young officer's vision. They followed through with the matching of dollars. Often they were not sure where the money would come from. At the end of one year, the officers borrowed ten thousand dollars to give away because they had faith in the basic principle that when the outgo meets with God's approval, God will provide the income needed.[8]

Vision to Risk

In the Old Testament, the Year of Jubilee came every fiftieth year. The Jubilee ideal called for letting the land lie fallow, the remission of all debts, the liberation of slaves, and the return of family property to its original owner. Jubilee represented the kind of daring vision called for on the part of God's people. Risky? Yes.

The fourth chapter of Luke describes Jesus' inauguration of his public ministry. When he returned to his home synagogue in Nazareth he rose to read from Scripture. The text he chose was Isaiah 61:1-2:

> "The spirit of the Lord is upon me,
> because he has anointed me to preach
> good news to the poor.
> He has sent me to proclaim release
> to the captives
> and recovering of sight to the blind,
> to set at liberty those who are oppressed,
> to proclaim the acceptable year of the Lord."
> (Luke 4:18-19)

---

8. Adaptation of an account in Charlie W. Shedd, *The Exciting Church Where They Give Their Money Away* (Waco, TX: Word Books, 1975), pp. 14-15.

After reading, Jesus announced, "Today this scripture has been fulfilled in your hearing" (Luke 4:21). That was risky. The crowd grew angry and tried to kill him. "Jesus had identified himself and his ministry with the whole Old Testament tradition of God's deliverance of those forced into the margins of human existence."[9] "To proclaim the acceptable year of the Lord" was to announce the Jubilee year. The placement of this statement at the beginning of Jesus' ministry strongly implies that we are to read his whole life and work in this manner.[10]

Jesus' life and ministry made these words real. Jesus did associate with and minister to the poor, the captives, the blind, and the oppressed. "He befriended society's outcasts, tax collectors, prostitutes, lepers, lunatics, and poor people."[11] In short, he took risks and he was criticized. As a matter of fact, he was crucified!

Yet we tend to be bound by the restrictive mold of the age in which we live. William Keucher illustrated this concern in his words about a man who had the task of blowing the noon whistle at the factory where he worked:

> [The man] made it a point to check his watch every morning with the most accurate chronometer in a certain jeweler's window. One day out of curiosity he stepped inside the jewelry store and asked the owner if his chronometer was set by Western Union, Arlington Time Signal, or Naval Observatory Time. Surprised at the question, the jeweler replied that he did not use any of those sources; he simply set his chronometer by the factory whistle that blew every day at noon![12]

The great need of our time is for men and women individually, and the church collectively, to envision themselves as stewards of the gospel of Jesus Christ and to take the risks neces-

9. Bruce C. Birch and Larry L. Rasmussen, *The Predicament of the Prosperous* (Philadelphia: Westminster Press, 1978), p. 90.

10. Ibid.

11. Ibid.

12. William F. Keucher, *An Exodus for the Church: From Yesterday to Tomorrow* (Valley Forge, PA: Judson Press, 1973), pp. 78-79.

sary to break out of restrictive molds and to live out the implications of the Kingdom of God.

When Jesus told his disciples that the gates of hell would not prevail against the church, he did not mean that the church is safely protected behind its walls so that the gates of hell cannot destroy the church as it stands in isolation, retreating from attacking forces.

> To look at the text . . . is to recognize that the gates of hell represent the stationary aspects of the picture, and it is the church which is to be the moving, mobile force. The church can only attack; the gates of hell are on the defensive.[13]

When the church goes on the offensive, people will have a vision of the ministry of the church as their own ministry, not simply the ministry of an institution, and they will provide the funds needed. People will support their own ministry, and with more than money alone.

"What I have to do," said Paul Tournier, "is to put my signature at the foot of a blank page on which I will accept whatever God wishes to write. I cannot predict what he will put on this blank contract as my life proceeds—but I give my signature today."[14] When we realize that we are the treasure for whom Jesus died, we will treasure doing God's will, at whatever risk.

> Love so amazing, so divine,
> Demands my soul, my life, my all.

The Journey

You are called to participate in the purpose of God, using and risking the resources that God provides. But for whom do you

---

13. Ibid., p. 98.

14. Paul Tournier, *The Adventure of Living* (New York: Harper & Row, 1965), p. 195, as quoted by Keucher in *An Exodus for the Church*, p. 120.

reach out in risk? In Part III and in the next chapter you will explore this question as the journey continues.

Questions and Suggestions
for Individual Reflection and Action

1. What is the greatest risk that you or your family ever took? What were the consequences—positive and negative?

2. What is the greatest risk that your congregation ever took? What were the consequences—positive and negative? Reflect on any parallels between the risk taken by you or your family and the risk taken by your congregation. What conclusions, if any, can be drawn?

3. In light of the parable and as a Christian steward, what is worth your risking everything for?

4. Consider and write down what would enable you to take such a risk. As your plan continues to develop, incorporate into it your willingness to take such risk.

5. As a steward of the gospel, what risks can/should your congregation be willing to take? For what purpose should these risks be taken? What recommendations might you make to the proper congregational officials or group?

PART III

Reaching Out

As a Christian steward, you are called to use and risk resources in order to reach out to others. "Others" includes both those persons with whom you can easily identify and especially those who are "different," even those whom you may not like, who do not like you, or about whom you have fear. The reaching out is to be based on actual need, not on what you feel or think that the other person(s) may or may not deserve. Nor is the reaching out in care to be limited to human beings only. You are called to care for all dimensions of planet Earth, and space beyond.

Chapter 10

$\boxed{C}$aring for Others

Parable of the Samaritan   (Luke 10:25-37)

And behold, a lawyer stood up to put him to the test, saying,
"Teacher, what shall I do to inherit eternal life?" He said to him,
"What is written in the law? How do you read?" And he answered, "You shall love the Lord your God with all your heart,
and with all your soul, and with all your strength, and with all
your mind; and your neighbor as yourself." And he said to him,
"You have answered right; do this, and you will live."

But he, desiring to justify himself, said to Jesus, "And who
is my neighbor?" Jesus replied, "A man was going down from
Jerusalem to Jericho, and he fell among robbers, who stripped
him and beat him, and departed, leaving him half dead. Now by
chance a priest was going down that road; and when he saw him
he passed by on the other side. So likewise a Levite, when he
came to the place and saw him, passed by on the other side. But
a Samaritan, as he journeyed, came to where he was; and when
he saw him, he had compassion, and went to him and bound up
his wounds, pouring on oil and wine; then he set him on his
own beast and brought him to an inn, and took care of him. And
the next day he took out two denarii and gave them to the innkeeper, saying, 'Take care of him; and whatever more you spend,

I will repay you when I come back.' Which of these three, do you think, proved neighbor to the man who fell among the robbers?" He said, "The one who showed mercy on him." And Jesus said to him, "Go and do likewise."

Expressing Love to Others in Gratitude for God's Love and Forgiveness

One of the clear calls to you as a Christian steward is to give yourself in deeds and acts of love to other persons, especially those who are "different" from you. The parable of the Samaritan (Luke 10:25-37) describes caring and the giving of time and money. "But a Samaritan . . . had compassion, and went to him and bound up his wounds."

*   *   *

Jesus' parable of the Samaritan is one of the best known, yet perhaps least understood of the parables. For many centuries, it was understood primarily as an allegory, in which each term was a code for an idea, so that the parable had to be decoded term by term. For example, C. H. Dodd recorded St. Augustine's famed interpretation of this parable:

> A certain man went down from Jerusalem to Jericho; Adam himself is meant; Jerusalem is the heavenly city of peace, from whose blessedness Adam fell; Jericho means the moon, and signifies our mortality, because it is born, waxes, wanes, and dies. Thieves are the devil and his angels. Who stripped him, namely, of his immortality; and beat him, by persuading him to sin; and left him half-dead, because in so far as man can understand and know God, he lives, but in so far as he is wasted and oppressed by sin, he is dead; he is therefore called half-dead. The priest and Levite who saw him and passed by, signify the priesthood and ministry of the Old Testament, which could profit nothing for salvation. Samaritan means Guardian, and therefore the Lord Himself is signified by this name. The binding of the wounds is the restraint of sin. Oil is the comfort of good hope; wine the exhortation to work with fervent spirit. The beast is the flesh in which He deigned to come to us. The being set upon the beast is belief in the incarnation of Christ. The inn is the Church, where travellers returning to their heavenly country are refreshed after

pilgrimage. The morrow is after the resurrection of the Lord. The two pence are either the two precepts of love, or the promise of this life and of that which is to come. The innkeeper is the Apostle (Paul). The supererogatory [beyond-the-expected] payment is either his counsel of celibacy, or the fact that he worked with his own hands lest he should be a burden to any of the weaker brethren when the Gospel was new, though it was lawful for him "to live by the Gospel."[1]

Helping Others

Today few, if any, persons would offer an elaborate allegorical interpretation such as Augustine's. The current trend is to interpret this parable as one that teaches us that we must be willing to offer help to a person in need. In fact, many governmental units in North America have adopted so-called "Good Samaritan" laws that exempt a physician or other medical personnel from any liability if he or she extends emergency first aid to a person who has been injured or suddenly stricken ill. Such an interpretation represents a very limited, even innocuous, understanding of the story of the Samaritan, since the intent of such laws is to reduce the element of risk to the person offering help. Is this what Jesus intended when he told this story?

Risking for Others

The parable of the Samaritan is not simply a story about giving first aid to someone in distress. That simply treats symptoms. The parable is a story about taking risks. The priest and the Levite in the parable would have been taking some degree of risk if either

1. C. H. Dodd, *The Parables of the Kingdom*, rev. ed. (New York: Charles Scribner's Sons, 1961), pp. 1-2, as taken by Dodd from *Quaestiones Evangeliorum*, II, 19, slightly abridged.

of them had chosen to stop and render aid to the wounded victim. The Samaritan did take risks, however.

- The robbers could have remained nearby and attacked anyone stopping to render aid.
- Another passer-by could have thought the Samaritan was robbing the victim.
- The victim could have been faking injury so as to lure any would-be helper into a trap.
- The victim could have rejected the Samaritan's help because he was "different."
- The Samaritan risked being rejected by his fellow Samaritans if they learned that he had helped a despised Jew.
- The helper risked being late for an appointment as he took time to give first aid and then arrange for the further care of the victim.
- The helper risked depleting his resources as he paid for care for the victim, and then promised to pay even more if it were needed.

Who Are the Others?

Clearly, the story is one of risk taking. But is that the primary point? To answer this question, we need to look at the setting and the question that prompted Jesus to tell the story.

A lawyer had asked Jesus a question in order to test him. "Teacher, what shall I do to inherit eternal life?" Jesus replied with a question, "What is written in the law? How do you read?" When the lawyer answered, "You shall love the Lord your God with all your heart, and with all your soul, and with all your strength, and with all your mind; and your neighbor as yourself," Jesus said to him, "You have answered right; do this, and you will live." But the man, desiring to justify himself, said to Jesus, "And who is my neighbor?" The story, then, was Jesus' answer to the question, "Who is my neighbor?"

The question was asked from the context of the Jewish law.

William Barclay noted that the Sabbath law stated that if, on the Sabbath, a wall were to collapse on a passer-by, enough could be cleared to see whether the injured man were a Jew or a gentile. If a Jew, he could be rescued; if a gentile, he must be left to suffer.[2]

A closer look at the parable reveals the essential point that Jesus was making as he answered the question, "Who is my neighbor?"

The victim in the story was on his way from Jerusalem to Jericho. He was traveling on a

> thief-infested stretch of rocky mountain road, a long, lonely twenty miles crowded with caves and danger. Jesus and his audience had made the trip many times. The route . . . had been nicknamed "The Bloody Pass." This traveler was ambushed, stripped of everything, beaten to a bloody pulp, and left to die a crimson wreck by the roadside.[3]

The first man to pass by the victim was a priest; the second was a Levite. Both were leaders in their religion—the religion shared by them with the dying victim who lay along the side of the road. But they passed on by. Perhaps they thought the victim was already dead and beyond their help. According to Jewish ritual, anyone who touched a dead body was considered unclean for seven days (Num. 19:11). If the victim were dead and was touched by a priest or a Levite, that priest or Levite would not have been permitted to carry out ritual responsibilities in the temple. Ritual was set above human need.

Then comes the telling twist in the story. A third man—a Samaritan—arrived on the scene. No one expected the third person to be a despised Samaritan. The words "priest," "Levite," and "Israelite," taken together, were frequently used to describe the Hebrew people. As the story unfolded, everyone assumed that the third person passing by would be an Israelite. Of all the substitu-

2. William Barclay, *And Jesus Said: A Handbook on the Parables of Jesus* (Philadelphia: Westminster Press, 1970), p. 82.

3. David A. Redding, *The Parables He Told* (Westwood, NJ: Fleming H. Revell, 1962), p. 119.

tions that Jesus could have made, none could have startled the crowd and the lawyer more than the use of a hated Samaritan.

It is well known that Samaritans and Jews despised one another. The quarrel had been going on for centuries, dating back to the destruction of the Northern Kingdom and its capital at Samaria. The Jews who were not deported by the invading army had intermarried with the foreigners who had been brought in. In so doing, they had lost their racial purity in the eyes of the Jews who did not intermarry. They were considered to be "half-breeds"—lower than gentiles. When Jesus mentioned the arrival of a Samaritan in the story, his listeners were sure that the villain in the story had arrived on the scene. It is hard today for us to imagine the shock that was felt as the hearers realized that the Samaritan was the hero of the story.

When I grew up in the state of Texas, so-called Jim Crow laws were in full force. Based on these laws, there was racial segregation at almost every level of society. In department stores, there were two types of drinking fountains (for white and for "colored") and four types of rest rooms (classified both by gender and by race). On buses and streetcars, moveable signs indicated clearly where persons of each race were to be seated. Schools were segregated. Twenty years after I graduated from high school in Dallas, I met a black man, Charles V. Willie, in Syracuse, New York. We discovered that we had lived about two miles apart in Dallas and had graduated from high school in the same year. But because of "Jim Crow," we did not meet in our high school years. My life was deprived of the opportunity to know this outstanding Christian leader twenty years sooner.

Clarence L. Jordan of Koinonia Farm, Americus, Georgia, captured the sense of surprise and shock felt by Jesus' hearers when he offered an interpretation of the parable, set in the context of the southern United States.[4] In Jordan's version, Jesus' dialogue is with an adult Bible class teacher who had been lis-

4. Clarence Jordan, *The Cotton Patch Version of Luke and Acts: Jesus' Doings and the Happenings* (New York: Association Press, 1969), pp. 46-47.

tening to Jesus and tested him by asking, "Doctor, what does one do to be saved?"

Jesus asked him what was his interpretation of what the Bible said. His answer? "Love the Lord your God with all your heart, soul, physical strength, and mind, and love your neighbor as yourself."

Jesus told him that he was correct, and that if he would make a practice of doing this, he would be saved. In an effort to save face, the Bible class teacher stammered, "But . . . just who is my neighbor?"

Jesus' response was a story set along the route from Atlanta to Albany, Georgia. A white man was traveling along this route and was held up by robbers. Taking his wallet and new suit, they beat him and drove off in his car, leaving him lying unconscious by the roadway.

A white preacher came driving along, took in the situation, and sped away. A white gospel song leader drove by and did the same.

A black man came by and was moved to tears by the sight of the man in need. He washed and dressed the man's wounds as best he could and drove him to a hospital in Albany. There he asked the nurse to take care of "this white man" and left with her the only two dollars he had. He requested that she keep track of the man's bill and, if he couldn't pay it, he would on his next payday.

Jesus then asked the Bible teacher a gut-wrenching question: "If you had been the victim of those robbers, who of the three would you consider to have been your neighbor?"

Jordan then painted a picture of a stammering, cornered Bible class teacher who finally answered, "Why, of course, the nig—I mean, er . . . well, er . . . the one who treated me kindly."

And Jesus said to him, "Well, then, you get on going and start living like that!"

While leading a church retreat on the subject of stewardship, I divided the participants into small groups, with each group asked to create a contemporary role play of Jesus' parable of the

Samaritan. When we reconvened, several of the groups gave interesting, though rather predictable presentations. One group, however, really "hit the nail on the head" in conveying the startling impact this parable must have had on those who heard Jesus speak the words. Not surprisingly, the first two persons who passed by the victim were a pastor and a deacon. The third person to travel by was a young Iranian student on a motorcycle. That got everyone's attention! The Iranian, though despised by most Americans, was the one who stopped and helped the robbery victim. The "neighbor" was not simply someone who lived nearby nor even someone "of the same kind" as the victim. He was different. He was despised by the people who were like the victim.

It is clear that the Christian steward must not only be willing to take risks, as we saw in the previous chapter, but must also be willing to take risks for persons who are quite "different" from him/herself. This means we are called to help persons who are despised by us, or by our society.

More Than Individuals

Nor can we be content with thinking only in terms of helping individuals. In the Bible, personal realities are never divorced from social and historical realities.

Consider these words of Jim Wallis:

> God did not give the Americans half the world's resources so that we could be good stewards of it; rather, the Americans have stolen those goods from the poor. Unless we are willing to stand with the oppressed by first breaking our attachment to wealth and comfort, all our talk of justice will be sheer hypocrisy. The stating of principles and good intentions, the denunciations of crying injustices, the endless declarations will lack any weight or moral authority apart from a deep awareness of our responsibility before God and our hungry neighbors.[5]

5. Jim Wallis, *Agenda for Biblical People: A New Edition* (San Francisco: Harper & Row, Publishers, 1984), pp. 66-67.

True love is more than emotion. It is caring action, extended to any person in need, without regard to the personal feelings of the helper. It is more than having pity, or feeling sorry for someone who has fallen into a pit. It is more than expressing sympathy. It is actually getting down into the pit and helping the person out. And it doesn't matter whether or not you know the person, how you may feel, or how dangerous the mission is.

Malcolm Muggeridge described experiencing such caring action in a visit with Mother Teresa:

> Accompanying Mother Teresa, as we did, to these different activities for the purpose of filming them—to the Home for the Dying, to the lepers and unwanted children, I found I went through three phases. The first was horror mixed with pity, the second compassion pure and simple, and the third, reaching far beyond compassion, something I had never experienced before—an awareness that these dying and derelict men and women, these lepers with stumps instead of hands, these unwanted children, were not pitiable, repulsive or forlorn, but rather dear and delightful; as it might be, friends of long standing, brothers and sisters. How is it to be explained—the very heart and mystery of the Christian faith? To soothe those battered old heads, to grasp those poor stumps, to take in one's arms those children consigned to dustbins, because it is his head, as they are his stumps and his children, of whom he said that whosoever received one such child in his name received him.[6]

An interesting question is: With whom in the parable do you identify? Most of us tend to answer: "The Samaritan." But consider some other possibilities:

- The lawyer—pious, studied, rehearsed, pretending;
- The victim—startled, wounded;
- The robbers—violent and greedy;
- The priest—more concerned about religious rules, duties, and customs than about risking caring concern;

6. Malcolm Muggeridge, *Something Beautiful for God*, quoted by Rueben P. Job and Norman Shawchuck in *A Guide to Prayer for Ministers and Other Servants* (Nashville: Upper Room, 1983), p. 233.

- The Levite—an exclamation point on the priest;
- The innkeeper—willing to help, if the price is right;
- And finally, the Samaritan—heroic, though despised.

Perhaps, at one time or another, you identify with most or even all of these persons.

The Journey

The parable is about far more than first aid or human kindness. Just as God's love is spontaneous, unqualified, and never limited by the rules of religion, so God wants you to love others. Only in defending the poor and weak can justice and order be established in society. The journey of the Christian steward involves taking risks on behalf of others—even those whom you may not like, or those who do not like you. As the next chapter will show, it involves reaching out to those who do not "deserve" help.

Questions and Suggestions for Individual Reflection and Action

1. In your community, who is the neighbor, the "other," to whom you as a Christian steward are to reach out? Make a list of possibilities for prayerful consideration.

2. Are there specific courses of action which you, possibly with others in your congregation or community, could take to reach out?

3. What steps would have to be taken? What resources would be needed? With whom might you consult? What recommendations or inquiries might you make?

4. Consider prayerfully how such outreach would be part of your journey as a Christian steward and incorporate this into your plan.

Chapter 11

Getting What You Deserve

Parable of the Laborers in the Vineyard
(Matthew 20:1-16)

"For the kingdom of heaven is like a householder who went out early in the morning to hire laborers for his vineyard. After agreeing with the laborers for a denarius a day, he sent them into his vineyard. And going out about the third hour he saw others standing idle in the market place; and to them he said, 'You go into the vineyard too, and whatever is right I will give you.' So they went. Going out again about the sixth hour and the ninth hour, he did the same. And about the eleventh hour he went out and found others standing; and he said to them, 'Why do you stand here idle all day?' They said to him, 'Because no one has hired us.' He said to them, 'You go into the vineyard too.' And when evening came, the owner of the vineyard said to his steward, 'Call the laborers and pay them their wages, beginning with the last, up to the first.' And when those hired about the eleventh hour came, each of them received a denarius. Now when the first came, they thought they would receive more; but each of them also received a denarius. And on receiving it they grumbled at the householder, saying, 'These last worked only one hour, and you have made them equal to us who have borne the burden of the day and the scorching heat.' But he replied to one of them, 'Friend, I am doing you no wrong; did you not agree with me for a denarius? Take what belongs to you, and go; I choose to give to this last as I give to you. Am I not allowed to do what I choose with what belongs to me? Or do you begrudge my generosity?' So the last will be first, and the first last."

Being Concerned about What People Need

As you help other persons, you are called to do so on the basis of need. The parable of the laborers in the vineyard (Matt. 10:1-16) describes workers who are paid according to their need, not what they deserve or have "earned." "I choose to give this last as I give to you."

*   *   *

Fair or Not Fair

"Unfair! That's not fair!" How often have you heard a young child call out these words? "Unfair" is one of the most common protests in the English language. The ideas of "fair play," "fair wages," and "fair practice" arouse our deepest emotions. Anything that violates our sense of what is fair can touch off a passionate protest.

The question of what is fair underlies many of the disputes that disrupt our society:

- Should the community control the public schools?
- What is fair pay for police officers, fire fighters, and garbage collectors?
- Are we being fair to children, to older people, to minority groups?
- What is fair taxation?
- Why do union members get paid such high wages?
- Why doesn't business consider anything except making a profit?

The word "unfair" turns up again and again in speeches, pamphlets, and picket signs. If the word "justice," used so much in the Bible, means anything, we must be concerned when such questions are raised. If we are honest, though, we will admit that often we descend from the platform of calm arbitration when it is our own interests that are in jeopardy.

The Eyes of Faith

One of the traits of the Christian steward is to be able to look at the world with the eyes of faith, that is, with a Christian perception of reality. But this is not an easy gift to acquire.

Jesus used parables to help men and women see the world with the eyes of faith—to subvert the view of the world that we ordinarily have. John H. Westerhoff III said:

> If you are not feeling very uncomfortable after you have read a parable in the Bible, just assume that you did not get it. Its function is to turn your life upside down and get you very upset. And most people are not upset about parables. That means that they did not get it.[1]

What Happened to Justice?

Consider the parable of the workers in the vineyard, as told by Jesus. Early in the morning, a householder went out to hire laborers for his vineyard. He agreed with a group of workers that he would pay them one denarius for a day's work and sent them into the vineyard. At midmorning he hired some more workers, telling them, "Whatever is right I will give you." He did the same at noon, at midafternoon, and late in the afternoon. When the day ended, the owner told his steward to pay each worker, beginning with the last, up to the first. All eyes were on the steward. What would he pay those who worked only the last hour of the day? A wave of surprise and confusion swept over the group as they observed the one-hour workers being paid a denarius. This

1. John H. Westerhoff III in a conference sponsored by American Baptist Churches of New York State in May 1982.

could mean only one of two things: either the others would be paid more, or, perish the thought, everyone would be paid the same. But there was optimism. Perhaps those who worked twelve hours would be paid twelve denarii. But optimism turned to anxiety, then fear, and finally anger, as the workers hired at midafternoon, at noon, and at midmorning each received one denarius. When the steward placed a denarius in the hand of one who worked a full day, the anger erupted. "You have made them equal to us who have borne the burden of the day and the scorching heat" (Matt. 20:12). William Barclay noted that there were certain times in Palestine when this story could actually have happened:

> By the middle of September the rains came and it was always a race with the weather to get the crop in. At such a time every available man would be pressed into service. The Jewish day ran from 6 a.m. to 6 p.m. The hours when the men were engaged were therefore 6 a.m., 9 a.m., 12 midday, 3 p.m. and finally 5 p.m. At the time of the harvest . . . it was quite possible that the owner of a vineyard would employ men as late as 5 o'clock in the evening. The denarius was the normal day's wage for a working man.[2]

You may well ask, "What sense does it make? What about 'an honest day's work for an honest day's pay'? Whatever happened to plain, ordinary justice? What happens to balance sheets, profit, and loss?" On the basis of this story, you would conclude that it is just as well to eat, drink, and be merry, or lounge around in bed all day, or use your wits and training to get all you can, to make your name and perhaps even a fortune.

None of this sits very well with a tit-for-tat world of balance sheets and profit and loss. We are used to a system where you have to do something if you expect to get something. If you want a driver's license, you must first pass the written and road tests. If you want a diploma, you must pass the exams and fulfill the re-

2. William Barclay, *And Jesus Said: A Handbook on the Parables of Jesus* (Philadelphia: Westminster Press, 1970), p. 162.

quirements. If you want financial security, you must save and invest your money wisely. This is the way we are used to operating.

But in the parable, this tit for tat falls apart. What happened to the bargain made by the first worker? Notice that the promised reward is still there. He was promised a denarius, and he received a denarius.

God's Generosity

The parable is a striking picture of God's generosity, giving without regard to the measures of strict justice. The "setting in life" is to be found in the ministry of Jesus. C. H. Dodd wrote:

> The divine generosity was specifically exhibited in the calling of publicans and sinners, who had no merit before God. The Kingdom of God is like that. Such is Jesus' retort to the complaints of the legally minded who cavilled at Him as the friend of publicans and sinners.[3]

Listen to the parable again, this time in a North American version as given by John H. Westerhoff III:

> A group of young, white males, early in the morning, are hired at a high rate of pay. About noontime, the owner goes out and finds a group of women who really want to work. They have children, though. He convinces one of them to run the day care center, and hires the others. About 4:00 he goes out and finds some blacks and chicanos and others who in our society have more trouble getting jobs than others, and hires those. At quarter to five he goes out and finds a group of people forced to retire and hires all of them. Then he closes the place down and gives them all the same salary. As you might guess, the young, white males hired early in the morning don't think that's very right. The owner of the vineyard says, "Hey, why are you so upset about my generosity?"[4]

3. C. H. Dodd, *The Parables of the Kingdom*, rev. ed. (New York: Charles Scribner's Sons, 1961), p. 95.
4. Westerhoff in the May 1982 conference.

Westerhoff continued:

> This is subversion. We live in a reward and punishment world. We define justice as getting what you deserve. Everybody may not get it, but they ought to. The Gospel says that we do not get what we deserve. I might add, thank God. God does not give us what we deserve; he gives us what we need. And we are to treat others that way.
>
> Now that is revolutionary. Do you know anybody who lives that way? Sometimes church people get upset over the welfare system, because somebody might get something that they don't deserve.
>
> We carry this attitude over into churches. Kids memorize Bible verses, so we give them Bibles. Perhaps the kids who need the Bibles are the ones who don't know anything. We hand out gold stars to the kids who come regularly. The kids who need that [affirmation] are the ones who don't come.
>
> We don't seem to know how to give people what they need. We're always giving them what they deserve. And that's antithetical to God.[5]

A Dilemma

This parable presents us a dilemma. On the one hand, you can't deny the householder's right to be generous. On the other hand, you might say that he is cutting his throat as an employer. The next time, who will want to sign on to work at the beginning of the day? We tend to say that, if he is going to be legalistic with one, then he should be legalistic with all. Or, if he is generous with one, he should be generous with all. Fair is fair. The parable seems to place the steward in a terrible bind.

By analogy, if God accepts some on the basis of merit and others on the basis of forgiveness, the situation is similarly intolerable. Either all must work out their own salvation with fear

5. Ibid.

and trembling, or all must rejoice in the goodness and mercy of the Lord. There is no third possibility.

Perhaps, if you are feeling somewhat uneasy at these words, it will be helpful to recall the context in which Jesus told this parable. In Matthew 19, the story is told of the rich young ruler who came to Jesus asking, "Teacher, what good deed must I do, to have eternal life?" (Matt. 19:16). When Jesus told him to "sell what you possess and give to the poor, and you will have treasure in heaven; and come, follow me," he went away sorrowful (Matt. 19:21-22).

The disciples asked, "Who then can be saved?" (Matt. 19:25), and Peter said, "Lo, we have left everything and followed you. What then shall we have?" (Matt. 19:27). There you have it. Sacrifices here, but rewards to dazzle forever afterward. Not a bad bargain. There is an assumption in Peter's question that God's grace is like a commercial commodity that is acquired in proportion to what you lay upon the counter.

Jesus replied that "the kingdom of heaven is like a householder who went out early in the morning to hire laborers for his vineyard" (Matt. 20:1), and went on to tell the parable of the workers in the vineyard. Jesus was speaking about the nature of the Kingdom of God. But these come as hard words. The devout in every age are quick to resent those who seem to be rewarded in ways they do not deserve. Recall the resentment of the elder son toward his brother in the parable we called the prodigal father.

Justice and Mercy Brought Together

Notice that there is reward in the parable of the vineyard. The workers who worked all day received the reward that they had been promised. Life is not meaningless. Events do have consequences. But the consequences are ultimately dependent upon God, not upon you and me. The parable brings together the two pillars of Jewish ethics: justice and mercy.

The picture seems distorted to us only when we look at it with a calculating eye. The philosophy expressed in Matthew 25 is much better: "Lord, when did we see thee hungry and feed thee, or thirsty and give thee drink. . . ?" (Matt. 25:37). The answer comes, "As you did it to one of the least of these my brothers [and my sisters], you did it to me" (Matt. 25:40). Here there is no calculating, no expectation of reward. It is an act based on need, not on what the other person deserves!

Many years ago, when a famine was bringing misery in Russia, the writer Leo Tolstoy passed by a bridge in Moscow where many beggars gathered. They were on the verge of starvation and were asking for alms. Seeing a beggar, Tolstoy searched in his pocket for a coin, but discovered that he had nothing with him, not even a copper coin. Embarrassed, Tolstoy took the beggar's hands in his own and said, "I am sorry, brother. Don't be angry with me. I have nothing with me today." The thin face of the beggar became illuminated, and he said in reply, "But you called me brother—that was a great gift, sir."[6]

Throughout the Bible, God takes the side of the poor, the oppressed, and the forsaken. Jesus, in his ministry, demonstrated this again and again. Ultimately, it is why he was crucified.

The Journey

In your relationship with God, an arrangement of uncalculating love is the only possible arrangement. If you seek a tit-for-tat arrangement with God, your relationship with God, and with your neighbor, is poisoned at the spring. The notion that "what you believe is your own business" is contrary to the way the Bible reads life.

Two things are clear:

6. Adapted from Jun Ehara, "Weep No More My Lady," in *Thanks*Giving: Stewardship Sermons out of the Ethnic Minority Experience*, ed. J. LaVon Kincaid, Sr. (Nashville: Discipleship Resources, 1984), pp. 37-38.

1. You can trust in the absolute fairness of God. God will do what is right. "I will pay you a fair wage," the householder said in the parable. God sees the whole story, in the light of eternity.

2. But, God is more than fair. And here we touch the heart of the gospel. God does not simply give you your desserts. God gives you life that you cannot possibly deserve. God is not a celestial bookkeeper. The amazing kindness of God can burn bitterness and jealousy out of your heart. "Why be jealous because I am kind?" The most agonizingly unfair act in history was the crucifixion of Jesus. Thank God that God did not calculate that Jesus did not deserve to die, or that you did not deserve to have Jesus die for you. As a Christian steward, you can rejoice that God gave you what you needed, not what you deserved. Thank God!

The next chapter will explore the dimensions of your accountability as a steward of the Earth.

Questions and Suggestions for Individual Reflection and Action

1. How do you respond to the concept that God gives people what they need, not what they deserve? Is this "justice"?

2. How can you, as a Christian steward, follow God's example of reaching out in an uncalculating love?

3. How would your life be different if you adopted a lifestyle of receiving and giving uncalculated love? What steps would have to be taken? What resources would be needed?

4. Continue the process of integrating your earlier reflections and planning with your current thoughts. Be open to new leadings and understandings that God may give to you on your journey as a Christian steward.

Chapter 12

Care for the Earth and Beyond

Parable of the Absentee Landlord
(Matthew 21:33-41)

"Hear another parable. There was a householder who planted a vineyard, and set a hedge around it, and dug a wine press in it, and built a tower, and let it out to tenants, and went into another country. When the season of fruit drew near, he sent his servants to the tenants, to get his fruit; and the tenants took his servants and beat one, killed another, and stoned another. Again he sent other servants, more than the first; and they did the same to them. Afterward he sent his son to them, saying, 'They will respect my son.' But when the tenants saw the son, they said to themselves, 'This is the heir; come, let us kill him and have his inheritance.' And they took him and cast him out of the vineyard, and killed him. When therefore the owner of the vineyard comes, what will he do to those tenants?" They said to him, "He will put those wretches to a miserable death, and let out the vineyard to other tenants who will give him the fruits in their seasons."

Caring for Planet Earth and Space
as Part of God's Creation

Part of creation entrusted to you as a steward is planet Earth. The parable of the absentee landlord (Matt. 21:33-41) tells the story of servants who misappropriate land given to them in trust, even killing the son of the owner in their attempt to gain ownership. "Come, let us kill him and have his inheritance."

*   *   *

"This is *mine!*" These words are often heard among siblings. The instinct for "turf protection" is very strong, even within a family setting. "What were you doing in my room?" "Why did you take my sweater?" "You didn't use my lipstick, did you?" A strong sense of ownership is built into our common daily experiences. When a new baby is born into a family, an older brother or sister may feel that the parents' time and attention is no longer directed toward him or her. Resentment and anger may be responses to the perceived invasion of turf. Usually, with patience, love, understanding, and communication, such problems can be resolved within the family setting. "Being family" can overcome many obstacles.

Turf Protection

"Turf protection" does not end as humans leave the family setting, however. In the work setting, for example, you may be upset if someone who is not authorized to do so enters your office or opens a desk drawer. If another employee or department takes on a responsibility that you feel belongs to you or to your department, tension begins to build.

Daily experiences offer many other examples. You do not like it if another person gets "in line" ahead of you. If someone sits in your accustomed seat on the bus or pew in the church, you may feel irritated, even though you know there is no good reason why you should. Such feelings of "turf protection" can erect barriers to a newcomer coming to a church or to a group within a church.

In other settings, "turf protection" creates bureaucratic "red tape," causing delays, inefficiencies, and injustices in institutions, business, industry, and government. Nations protect their turf, and wars result.

Who Owns the Land?

In the parable of the absentee landlord, Jesus described a magnificent vineyard that belonged to a landowner who had left the vineyard to be worked by tenants and had gone into another country. The tenants were accountable for the fruits of the vineyard. Soon, however, the tenants began to think of the vineyard as belonging to them. "We've done all the work. There certainly wouldn't be any harvest without us. This land is ours. Why should we share any of the harvest with the owner?" When the owner sent servants to get his fruit, the tenants "beat one, killed another, and stoned another" (Matt. 21:35). When the owner sent more servants, they received the same treatment. Then the owner sent his son, thinking "They will respect my son" (Matt. 21:37). But they killed the son also.

Of course, you are shocked when you hear such a story. But is it possible that humans are behaving similarly when we treat the planet Earth as "our vineyard"—to do as we wish with the fruits and even the vineyard itself? Do we forget that "The earth is the Lord's"?

For many years, most of us who lived in North America nurtured a "no-limits" mentality. For example, in 1967 Buckminster Fuller wrote:

> Humanity's mastery of vast, inanimate, inexhaustible energy sources and the accelerated doing more with less of sea, air, and space technology has proven Malthus to be wrong. Com-

prehensive physical and economic success for humanity may now be accomplished in one-fourth of a century.[1]

Such expectations were not realistic. We thought we could go to the moon, feed the world's hungry, win the war on poverty, and end the threat of war.

> In July 1969 . . . U.S. astronauts took "one giant leap for mankind" onto the moon. President [Richard M.] Nixon called it "the greatest week in the history of the world since creation!" An official of NASA (National Aeronautics and Space Administration) said it demonstrated we were "masters of the universe." Millions felt it meant we could do whatever we set our minds to do.[2]

Fragile and Finite

In more recent years, we have begun to realize that this planet Earth is not ours to do with in any way we please. More and more we are realizing that the Earth is fragile and finite. Though God will provide the resources we need, this does not mean that we should assume that physical resources should be wasted. In the wilderness, you will recall, God gave the Israelites the manna they needed, day by day.

The most vital of all resources on this planet is water. Two-thirds of our body's weight and nine-tenths of its volume is water. That is why water is essential to life. A human being may survive for up to two months without food, but will die within three days without water. Consider these facts about water:

- Over half the people in the Third World do not have clean water to drink.

1. Buckminster Fuller, as quoted by Bruce C. Birch and Larry L. Rasmussen in *The Predicament of the Prosperous* (Philadelphia: Westminster Press, 1978), p. 22.

2. Ibid., pp. 22-23.

- Three quarters have no sanitation at all.
- More than three quarters of human illness is related to the lack of clean drinking water and sanitation.
- When water must be fetched from a well or river, people consume an average of 12 liters [approximately 3 U.S. gallons] a day. When it is freely available from household taps, people consume a staggering 165 liters [approximately 44 U.S. gallons] each a day—or more.
- The cost of supplying clean water to every community in the world has been estimated at $27 billion a year:
    —one quarter of what the world spends each year on alcohol;
    —one-third of what is spent on cigarettes;
    —one-twentieth of what the world spends each year on arms.[3]

In fact, all material resources are limited. It is increasingly clear that continued growth in demand is on a collision course with the amount of material resources available.

Contributing Factors

Population is a significant factor in this interaction. A growth rate of 2% per year, which is the present rate of world population increase,[4] means that the world population would double in barely 35 years. In only 56 years it would triple, and within 117 years it would be ten times as great. It is apparent that at some time in the future the population growth rate must move to zero. What is not known is what population level the material resources of planet Earth can sustain.

One factor in the population growth rate is the fact that people are living longer. For the first time in history, a new genera-

3. Information gleaned from the August page of the Church World Service's *1984 Third World Calendar.*
4. Birch and Rasmussen, *The Predicament of the Prosperous,* p. 24.

tion—the over 60s—is emerging. Total world population is expected to triple between 1950 and 2025. But the United Nations has predicted a fivefold increase in the population of the over 60s. From 1950 to 2025, the percentage of the world's population over age 60 is anticipated to grow from 8.5% to 13.7%. With this shift in what demographers call the "dependency ratio," efforts will have to be made to stress the productive involvement of the aged, not just their protection and care.[5]

We also know that the distribution of the population on the Earth is not even. If the present population of four and a half billion persons were represented as just one hundred persons, they would be as follows:

11 from Europe
 6 from the Soviet Union
 6 from North America
22 from China
16 from India
16 from the rest of Asia
 4 from the Middle East
 8 from Latin America and the Caribbean
10 from Africa
 1 from Australasia and the Pacific.

- Many are very young. 36 are under the age of 15. Only six are over 65.
- 20 people have a radio; five have a car; seven have a television set.
- Over the last year, there has been one death in the group. But there has also been one wedding. And three babies born.

Multiply these figures by 45 million and you have the actual population of the earth.[6]

5. Information gleaned from the June page of the Church World Service's 1984 Third World Calendar.

6. Information gleaned from the October page of the Church World Service's 1984 Third World Calendar.

The Earth, entrusted to our care by God (Gen. 1:28), is a marvelous work of God's creation, capable of meeting human needs if it is cared for properly. It is the "vineyard" God placed in our care. But it is not ours to plunder and pollute. Increasingly we are aware of the fragility of our environment on planet Earth.

For over forty years, since an atomic bomb was dropped over Hiroshima, Japan, inhabitants of our planet have lived in dread and fear of a *nuclear holocaust* that could kill hundreds of millions of persons and wreak havoc on the fragile planet Earth. These statistics emphasize the deadly danger that confronts humankind:

- The standard bomb today is one megaton.
- One megaton means seventy times the power of the bomb dropped on Hiroshima.
- It is the equivalent of one million tons of TNT.
- If you put that much TNT into boxcars, the train would be 200 miles long.
- Ten megatons is more than all the explosives used in World War II.
- Twenty megatons is more than all the explosives ever used![7]

With the announcement of the so-called "Star Wars" defense by the United States, the arena of possible nuclear explosions has expanded from the planet's surface and atmosphere to space. The Strategic Defense Initiative (SDI) has proposed placing defensive weaponry on hundreds of satellites to destroy incoming ICBM's. Estimates of the cost of such a system have been placed at $1 trillion.[8]

Such a defense would not have the advantage of being certain. "With tens of thousands of warheads raining down on the

7. Douglas John Hall, *The Steward: A Biblical Symbol Come of Age* (New York: Friendship Press, 1982), p. 117.

8. "The Star Warriors," *Newsweek* 105, no. 25 (June 17, 1985): 41.

United States, even a small leak would lead to destruction of the 'soft targets'—that is, human beings."[9]

Further complicating this strategy is the reality that the computer program controlling this defense

> "would require 10 million lines of error-free code." . . . Highly intricate computer programs never work right the first time. Because no software designer can anticipate every contingency, the only way to debug the Star Wars computers would be to test the entire system under the actual conditions it would encounter—that is, a war.[10]

Each of the factors mentioned has a major impact upon our fragile planet and its inhabitants. Taken together, they seem to be beyond human capability to cope. Yet God holds human beings accountable. (See Genesis 3.) Humans still bear the image of God. Every human being bears a stewardship responsibility. The Christian is privileged to know in a special way the meaning of the stewardship drama: knowing who is the Owner of the universe and the Ruler of life and what God is about in creation and redemption, in short, what it means to be a steward in the household of God.

Human Accountability

How then can Christians exercise accountability to God? What is the role of the church in the world of today? While there are no quick and easy answers to such questions, your identity as a Christian steward can provide some clues and a sense of direction. "Translating the stewardship of the Kingdom into the terms of our own context means, certainly, that we must be much more skeptical of worldly ideologies."[11]

In 1864, Chief Seattle responded to "the Great Chief in Washington" when the U.S. Government sent word that it

9. Ibid., pp. 41-42.
10. Ibid., pp. 42-45.
11. Hall, *The Steward*, p. 121.

wanted to buy his people's land. He recognized the reality that human beings do not own the Earth:

> How can you buy or sell the sky, the warmth of the land? The idea is strange to us.
>
> If we do not own the freshness of the air and the sparkle of the water, how can you buy them?
>
> Every part of this earth is sacred to my people. Every shining pine needle, every sandy shore, every mist in the dark woods, every clearing, and [every] humming insect is holy in the memory and experience of my people. The sap which courses through the trees carries the memories of the red man.
>
> The white man's dead forget the country of their birth when they go to walk among the stars. Our dead never forget the beautiful earth, for it is the mother of the red man. We are part of the earth and it is part of us. The perfumed flowers are our sisters; the deer, the horse, the great eagle, these are our brothers. The rocky crests, the juices in the meadows, the body heat of the pony, and man—all belong to the same family.
>
> So, when the Great Chief in Washington sends word that he wishes to buy the land, he asks much of us.[12]

Many practical things need to be done. You need to determine what they are within the context of your life and the stewarding community of which you are a part.

Yet there is an even more significant prior step: "We can determine that we shall not any longer be amongst those who are ambiguous about the world, who withdraw from it, and whose withdrawal results in 'an almost demonstrable loss to the world.'"[13]

This Land Is *God's* Land

God calls us to love the world as God loves it—not as "turf" to be protected for our sake, but as God's creation. "And God saw

---

12. Birch and Rasmussen, *The Predicament of the Prosperous*, p. 183.
13. Hall, *The Steward*, p. 122.

everything that he had made, and behold, it was very good" (Gen. 1:31).

A few years ago a heavy rain shower passed over the area where I live. A few minutes after it passed, at about 6:00 p.m., I went out into our yard and looked toward the east. There, for only the second time in my life, I saw a complete double rainbow, unbroken from horizon to horizon. How beautiful to see the brilliant colors of the primary rainbow, and to see the same colors, reversed and subdued, arching above in the secondary rainbow.

As I reflected on the magnificence of the view, my thoughts went to God's covenant with Noah as stated in Genesis 8 and 9. In that covenant God confirmed the orderliness and regularity of the seasons and promised that the earth would never again be destroyed by a universal flood. God designated the rainbow as a sign of this promise. Every rainbow after a storm, thus, is a token of God's sovereignty over the whole creation. Humankind is God's representative. This is a compelling description of our relationship to God as God's stewards. We are called, as stewards, to care for God's earth.

The double rainbow took on a new meaning for me. The primary rainbow symbolizes God's sovereignty over the earth and the promise of care and concern. The secondary rainbow, subdued and inevitably related to the primary rainbow, speaks to me of the Christian's responsibility as God's steward.

A Steward's Declaration

As a Christian steward who recognizes that the earth and the fullness thereof is entrusted to you by God, that you are called to be a steward of the earth and all its resources, and that your very life comes from God, consider the following action commitments:

1. I will commit myself to personal renewal through prayer, study of the Bible, and meditation.

2. I will commit myself to regular and responsible participation in a community of faith.
3. I will accept accountability to God, the Creator and Owner, for my treatment of the world.
4. I will commit myself to lead a life of creative simplicity and to share what God has entrusted to me with the world's poor.
5. I will join with others to help bring about a more just society in which each person has access to needed resources for physical, emotional, intellectual, and spiritual growth.
6. I will be accountable to God in my occupation, and in so doing I will seek to avoid the creation of or participation in products or services that harm others.
7. I will affirm God's gift of my body, and commit myself to its proper nourishment and physical well-being.
8. I will commit myself to examine my relations with others, and to attempt to relate in love and concern to others.[14]

The Journey

As a Christian steward, you are called to care for and be accountable for all of planet Earth and the surrounding space affected by human activity.

Let the prayer of Chief Yellow Lark speak to you at this point in your journey:

> Oh Great Spirit, whose voice I hear in the winds, and whose breath gives life to all the world, hear me.
>
> I come before You, one of Your many children. I am small and weak. I need Your strength and wisdom.
>
> Let me walk in beauty and make my eyes ever behold the

14. Adapted from Thomas G. Pettepiece, *Visions of a World Hungry*, quoted by Rueben P. Job and Norman Shawchuck in *A Guide to Prayer for Ministers and Other Servants* (Nashville: Upper Room, 1983), pp. 116-17.

red and purple sunset. Make my hands respect the things You have made, my ears sharp to hear Your voice.

Make me wise, so that I may know the things You have taught my people, the lesson You have hidden in every leaf and rock.

I seek strength, not to be superior to my brothers, but to be able to fight my greatest enemy—myself.

Make me ever ready to come to You with clean hands and straight eyes, so when life fades as a fading sunset, my spirit may come to You without shame.[15]

The next chapter brings you to a vital step in the steward's journey. In your journey as a steward, God calls you to envision. Your accountability as a steward is not to be undertaken haphazardly, but with creative wisdom.

Questions and Suggestions
for Individual Reflection and Action

1. Read and save news accounts that portray problems and/or solutions related to the earth and its finite resources.

2. Ask yourself, "As a Christian steward, how can I play a part in bringing about solutions to the depletion of resources and the pollution of the earth?" "What are the life-style implications for me and others?"

3. Recognizing that "the earth is the Lord's," what practical steps can you and others in your congregation and community take to address and help resolve problems related to care for the earth? What resources would be needed?

4. How do these steps relate to your journey as a Christian steward? Incorporate them into your developing plan.

15. Chief Yellow Lark from Seattle, "An Indian Prayer," printed on a bookmark by Bacone College, Muskogee, Oklahoma.

PART IV

REALITY AND GROWTH

As a Christian steward, you are not to use God's resources in a haphazard manner. God calls you to envision and to plan—to be shrewd, not in a negative sense, but in the positive sense of being wise and prudent. Risking is to be done with wisdom. Results are to be evaluated and plans revised as necessary. Your journey as a Christian steward is not static and inflexible. God is dynamic and God's creation is "in process." Consequently, you are called to grow and to change as God leads and calls you to new ministries.

Chapter 13

Shrewdness: Assessing Reality

Parable of the Unjust Steward (Luke 16:1-8)

He also said to the disciples, "There was a rich man who had a steward, and charges were brought to him that this man was wasting his goods. And he called him and said to him, 'What is this that I hear about you? Turn in the account of your stewardship, for you can no longer be steward.' And the steward said to himself, 'What shall I do, since my master is taking the stewardship away from me? I am not strong enough to dig, and I am ashamed to beg. I have decided what to do, so that people may receive me into their houses when I am put out of the stewardship.' So, summoning his master's debtors one by one, he said to the first, 'How much do you owe my master?' He said, 'A hundred measures of oil.' He said to him, 'Take your bill, and sit down quickly and write fifty.' Then he said to another, 'And how much do you owe?' He said, 'A hundred measures of wheat.' He said to him, 'Take your bill, and write eighty.' The master commended the dishonest steward for his prudence; for the sons of this world are wiser in their own generation than the sons of light."

Coming to Terms with Life's Realities

As you seek to fulfill the purpose of God, God calls you to be forthright and to engage in energetic planning. In short, it is a call for shrewdness, in the best meaning of that word. The parable of the unjust steward (Luke 16:1-8) describes the shrewdness of a dishonest steward. "The sons of this world are wiser in their own generation than the sons of light."

*   *   *

A Dishonest Steward

For many persons, Jesus' parable of the dishonest steward is one of the most troubling of all the parables. It is filled with "enticing dead-end possibilities."[1] Could Jesus have told a parable that praises dishonesty? Whom does the dishonest steward represent?

The story tells of a rich man who had a steward to whom he had entrusted his investments, the handling of his accounts, and the collection of interest due him. When reports came to the rich man that the steward was wasting his goods, the steward was called to accountability. He was told to turn in the account of his stewardship—he could no longer be steward. The response of the steward was to go to those who owed money to his employer, accept partial payment, and mark their accounts as paid in full. His reasoning was that, by accepting less than the full amount due, he would make friends of the debtors. The shocking point of the parable comes when the steward is *commended* for his prudent action.

---

1. Lloyd John Ogilvie, *Autobiography of God* (Glendale, CA: GL Regal Books, 1979), p. 200.

Praise for Prudence

Is Jesus telling his disciples to practice dishonesty? Is the dishonesty of the steward being lifted up as a model for the Christian? The answer to these two questions is "no." What then is the point of the parable? Why was the steward commended?

> This is about the boldest parable Christ ever told. But he is not commending that rascal's morals, but applauding his uncommon good sense. The rogue uses his crooked head to get ahead on earth, better than good men use theirs to get to heaven.[2]

It was for his prudence, his wisdom. He was able to focus on a planned course of action. He assessed the reality of the crisis facing him and acted with prompt foresight. This was shrewdness. Shrewdness, when it is exercised with compassion, is a mark of the steward.

On another occasion, when Jesus was sending out his twelve disciples, he told them that they were to be "wise as serpents and innocent as doves" (Matt. 10:16). The word translated "wise" here is the same word that is translated "prudent" in the parable. Forthrightness, strategic planning, and complete devotion to a purpose were being praised. Jesus admired prudence, wisdom, a "shrewdness-in-love" that is able to assess reality and deal with a crisis.

Tensions Surrounding Shrewdness

Many times Christians perceive a tension between wisdom or shrewdness on the one hand and "being harmless" on the other hand. Yet no tension need exist. The key lies in the answer to the question, "Who is the intended beneficiary of the action being planned?" If the primary beneficiary is oneself or one's group at the expense of others, then the planned action may be shrewd, but it is probably not harmless.

2. David A. Redding, *The Parables He Told* (Westwood, NJ: Fleming H. Revell, 1962), p. 111.

Examples of shrewdness exercised for selfish intent abound:

- A business or industry executive whose only concern is the bottom line and for whom the welfare of the employees, the customers, the larger society, and the environment is at best a secondary concern.
- A person in sports, entertainment, government, or some other field who gives great thought and calculation to the advancements of his or her career. Sacrifice, scheming, and study are freely invested for the anticipated career benefits. Fame and fortune beckon and shrewdness is the response.
- A criminal mastermind whose talents are used to steal from or injure others.
- A military leader who plans for wars of the future, forgetting about the danger, destructiveness, and pain of war.

A scepticism that a Christian can be "both shrewd and good" makes it difficult for many Christians to engage in planning or to take actions that they would construe to be shrewd. The result is that the church often fumbles in its efforts to fulfill the mission God has entrusted to it. Lack of planning and half-hearted attempts do not get the job done. The church may give up at just the point where a profit-making business organization would intensify its efforts.

> But they [the rascal and the debtors in Jesus' parable] were wholehearted in their rascality. The steward was willing to bend every effort to maintain his comfort. The debtors were willing to catch at any chance to cancel part of their debt. If Christians were as keen on their Christianity as these men were on their dubious business it would be a vastly different world. As Hugh Martin put it, "If they took as much trouble with their Christianity as they do in trying to reduce their handicap at golf or in growing their roses they would be much better people."[3]

3. William Barclay, *And Jesus Said: A Handbook on the Parables of Jesus* (Philadelphia: Westminster Press, 1970), p. 147.

Obstacles to Shrewdness

The Christian steward, however, may perceive many "obstacles" to shrewdness:

- Lack of confidence: "I don't have the skills needed to do planning."
- Uncertainty: "I'm not sure that it is right for me to try to plan for the future. After all, that's in God's hands. Nothing will really change."
- Hopelessness: "It really doesn't matter what I say or do."
- Apathy: "I have been beaten down so many times that I don't want to try again."
- Confusion: "I don't see how we can possibly establish priorities. Everything is so important."
- Fear of others' opinions: "If we make a decision about that issue, then somebody is going to be really upset. It's better if we put the matter off until another time."
- Fear of bureaucratic "red tape": "It's no use. No matter what we may decide, nothing will ever really happen. It takes forever for them to make a decision."
- Lack of courage: "That sounds pretty good, but I'm not sure we're ready to do that right now."
- Fear of change: "I don't think we're ready to consider doing that!" Or, the words that have been described as The Seven Last Words of the Church: "We never did it that way before."

Creative Planning

Despite these perceived obstacles, it is possible for a group of Christians to be as "wise as serpents and innocent as doves." Creative planning and strategizing can be an exciting process for a group, generating not only new ideas, but enthusiasm and "ownership" by the participants as well. When a group has wrestled with priorities and has agreed on an overarching purpose with goals, objectives, and action plans following in turn, and when that overarching purpose is perceived by the members of the group to be for the sake of God and not of mammon, powerful forces come into play.

I have had the privilege, on several occasions, of being part of such a group process. Results that we would not have thought possible came to pass through a combination of prayer, envisioning, and planning. A willingness to give of resources in ways hardly envisioned before took place. What were previously thought to be insurmountable barriers were overcome. Years later, participants recalled the experience with fondness.

Rusbuldt, Gladden, and Green list three reasons for planning: (1) to know where you're going; (2) to figure out how to get there; and (3) to know when you have arrived.[4] In an earlier work, they used a parable to illustrate the importance of these steps in effective planning:

> Two transportation firms, with an eye to profit, each launched a passenger ship to sail the oceans of the world. Both ships attracted customers. Each bustled with excitement and activity. For a time, both were profitable. One firm insisted on regular maintenance and from time to time added new types of service. These were costly and for several weeks each year this ship was in dry dock, cutting the number of its voyages and its firm's profits. The other company insisted their ship sail every week of the year, to return an uninterrupted profit from ticket sales. This it was able to do.
>
> Several years passed. Slowly a trend began to develop. Fewer people sailed on the year-round ship. The other ship, regularly dry-docked, continued to have all the passengers it could accommodate at each sailing. Conditions on the year-round ship finally reached the point where the owners were no longer able to make a profit by carrying passengers; their analysis of the changing sit-

4. Richard E. Rusbuldt, Richard K. Gladden, and Norman M. Green, Jr., *Key Steps in Local Church Planning* (Valley Forge, PA: Judson Press, 1980), p. 10.

uation soon forced them to convert the vessel from a passenger ship to one that carried only cargo.[5]

A short-term gain can lead to a long-term loss and disadvantage.

Furthermore, planning needs to be comprehensive, not piecemeal. Keucher illustrated this significant point in a humorous way:

> An inquisitive passenger [was] on the rear platform of a long train, slowly winding its way along a broad French river. He was puzzled by the signs which they passed. He knew they were not mileposts because they were always the same series—100—125—150. He concluded that they could not be speed-limit signs because, with those sharp curves, no engineer could be making a hundred miles an hour and keep the train on the track. Finally he asked a flagman, "What do those signs mean?" The flagman answered, "Car lengths. There are so many car lengths to the switch. If it is a lon ; train, the engineer can't see all of it at once around these lon ; curves. But he knows how many cars he has got in his train, ar d the signs tell him whether or not the last car is out of the siding. You see," the flagman concluded, "the engineer's got to know where his hind end is."[6]

The Journey

As a Christian steward, you are called to experience the totality of what it means to be a steward of God. The journey of the Christian steward involves more than a single step. It involves experiencing the joy of God's love; seeking to determine God's purpose in specific situations; acknowledging that God is ready to provide resources; being willing to accept those resources; and being willing to take risks in using those resources for other per-

5. Richard E. Rusbuldt, Richard K. Gladden, and Norman M. Green, Jr., *Local Church Planning Manual* (Valley Forge, PA: Judson Press, 1977), p. 23.

6. William E. Keucher, *An Exodus for the Church* (Valley Forge, PA: Judson Press, 1973), pp. 89-90.

sons and their needs, while exercising care for the planet on which you live.

All this is to be done "shrewdly," with wisdom and prudence, with planning based on the reality of your "setting in life" and the community of which you are a part.

But there is still more in the steward's journey. It is important that you remain open to growth and change. The journey does not end at any set point. You are called to listen for and respond to new challenges and understandings from God.

Questions and Suggestions for Individual Reflection and Action

1. Why are Christians sometimes charged with not having "common sense"? Are the charges justified? If so, in what way?

2. Ask yourself, "In my journey as a Christian steward, how can I combine shrewdness and caring love?"

3. In your ongoing planning for your journey, what remains to be done? If you have been working with the questions and suggestions at the end of each chapter, you may be near the point of implementing your plan. Begin (or continue) the process of combining your prayers, thoughts, studies, and actions with others. What questions or recommendations would you like to discuss? Is there a group in your congregation with whom you could pray, study, and work? If not, could you help start such a group? Whom might you contact?

Chapter 14

Growth and Change

Parables of the New Patch and the New Wine
(Luke 5:34-38)

And Jesus said to them, "Can you make wedding guests fast while the bridegroom is with them? The days will come, when the bridegroom is taken away from them, and then they will fast in those days." He told them a parable also: "No one tears a piece from a new garment and puts it upon an old garment; if he does, he will tear the new, and the piece from the new will not match the old. And no one puts new wine into old wineskins; if he does, the new wine will burst the skins and it will be spilled, and the skins will be destroyed. But new wine must be put into fresh wineskins."

Growing as God Works in Your Life

The steps mentioned in this book are not the whole of the journey of a Christian steward. You are called to grow and to change as God leads you. A vital sign of a Christian steward is the willingness to let the ferment of God's actions work freely in your life. The parables of the new patch and new wine (Luke 5:34-38) remind you that God can and does break forth with new revelation that demands new openness. "The new wine will burst the skins."

*　　　*　　　*

Change can be frightening. This is particularly true if an individual is basically content with the status quo in his or her life and sees no real need for change. Sometimes a Christian may rejoice in an experience with God that took place in the past, perhaps years or even decades before. That is good, if the rejoicing does not prevent that person from anticipating and seeking new experiences with God.

A Willingness to Change

One of the necessary marks of a Christian steward and of a church that is a faithful steward is a willingness to grow and to change. Our faith is to be dynamic, not static, because the journey of a Christian steward never reaches an end. This book has traced some of the major stepping stones in a steward's faith journey. However, it is never enough to say, "I have followed *the* steps; therefore I have fulfilled the obligations of Christian stewardship." The journey may involve touching base with certain steps more than once. It may involve learning that there are dimensions in the journey that were not recognized before and continuing the journey into heretofore unexplored territory. Just at the point that a Christian steward feels that he or she has reached land's end, God may call that person to launch out and learn of greater things ahead.

Nor is the church as steward called to security or isolation. On the contrary, the church is to be "on the move," a pilgrim church following the lead of the One who is the Head of the church—Jesus the Christ. Inevitably, the church will include people who are at different steps in their journey. This diversity is part of the rich texture of the church.

Openness to New Understandings

Jesus' twin parables of the new wine in old skins and the new patch on old cloth teach that whatever we may have learned of God in the past is not the whole of God's truth. The context of the parables, as given in Luke 5:17-33, shows that Jesus was speaking in response to the shock and confusion of the Pharisees about what Jesus had done and said. Jesus was challenging their experience and understanding of God. Their God was a God of history who did not speak and act in the present age. Thus, when Jesus healed a paralyzed man and said, "Your sins are forgiven you" (Luke 5:20), their experience and understanding of God was stretched to the breaking point. How could a rabbi from Nazareth be a channel of God's forgiveness?

Then Jesus called a tax collector named Levi to follow him. Tax collectors were hated and despised by the good citizens of Israel. After all, they not only gouged and cheated the people, they were in collusion with Rome. As a result, they were excluded from worship and the rights of their national and religious heritages. When Jesus accepted an invitation from Levi to meet some of his tax-gathering friends, the Pharisees and their scribes grumbled, "Why do you eat and drink with tax collectors and sinners?" (Luke 5:30).

As Jesus told the parables, he was taking familiar images and teaching new truths. In Jesus' time, the skin of a goat was coated with pitch and sealed to make a bag. Using the neck as an opening, the new wine, freshly pressed from the grapes, was poured in and the neck closed tightly. Then the process of fermentation began. The new skin, being fresh and flexible, could stretch and expand as the new wine fermented. By contrast, an old skin, already stretched to capacity, could not contain the new wine. The fermentation process would be sure to burst the old skin. [1]

The old way, the old covenant, the old understandings of the Pharisees were being burst by the fermentation of the process Jesus was setting in motion. And that fermentation process continues to this day in the journey of the Christian steward.

> The Lordship of Jesus Christ cannot be poured into the old skin of our settled personality structure, presuppositions about life, prejudices about people, plans for the future and predetermined ideas of what He will do or how we will respond. The dry, cracked bags of the past will burst; we will lose our cherished religion and Him as well.[2]

The world of the late twentieth century is undergoing rapid and significant technological change. This calls for change in the ways in which we organize ourselves—change in the systems and structures that put and hold things together.

But Bruce C. Birch and Larry L. Rasmussen envision *additional* needed change:

> Somewhat more surprising is the call for . . . a perception change, a change in how we see things. . . . There is one solid common conclusion: ours is a time in which change in perception is critical to any kind of humane future.[3]

What is a perception change? "It is change in how the world is viewed, or portions of it."[4]

---

1. The description of the process is adapted from Lloyd John Ogilvie, *Autobiography of God* (Glendale, CA: GL Regal Books, 1979), pp. 124-25.

2. Ibid., p. 125.

3. Bruce C. Birch and Larry L. Rasmussen, *The Predicament of the Prosperous* (Philadelphia: Westminster Press, 1978), p. 57.

4. Ibid., p. 58.

A Time of Profound Change

Such far-reaching change occurs only when the basic factors of vision and coercion are present.

> History's testimony is that the most far-reaching change comes only with the combination of strong pressures, from within and without, and a compelling vision. The lure of an alternative vision is not enough of itself. Nor is coercion alone a means of truly basic and long-lasting change. The combination of push and pull is required.[5]

Jorgen Randers concluded his work on the Limits to Growth report by writing that "probably only religion has the moral force to bring about [the necessary] change."[6]

The times are changing significantly. Evidences of change have been presented in this book. This time of transition is like a time between the times. Just as in the time of the New Testament, there is a sound of two different ages clashing. There is a recasting of the way in which things are perceived.

> The previous data and experiences are still there, of course. But they appear in a different light and comprise a new constellation. They are reordered.[7]

Perhaps because the change is so all-encompassing and pervasive, it is not fully realized how great the change is. When asking who discovered water, Marshall McLuhan "answered his own question by saying that while we don't know for sure, it probably wasn't a fish! A fish would be too immersed to notice. The fish would learn more about water the first time out."[8]

5. Willis W. Harman, "The Coming Transformation," *The Futurist* 11, no. 2 (April 1977): 106, as cited by Birch and Rasmussen in ibid., p. 73.

6. Jorgen Randers, "Global Limitations and Human Responsibility," in *To Create a Different Future*, ed. Kenneth Vaux (New York: Friendship Press, 1972), p. 32, as cited by Birch and Rasmussen in ibid., p. 60.

7. Ibid., p. 62.

8. Ibid., p. 65. The source of the McLuhan statement is not given.

Opportunity for change on such a scale is rare. George Lindbeck wrote that there have been "only a few periods in the last two thousand years of Christian history when changes comparable in magnitude to the present ones have been in process."[9] Some of the turning points he mentioned are the "transition from Judaism to Hellenism in the first few centuries, the shift on the part of the church from persecuted minority to imperial majority with Constantine, and the Reformation cataclysm."[10]

The Steward's Struggle

If we accept as reality that such a profound change is indeed taking place, what then is the role of the Christian steward and of the church as steward?

No detailed blueprint will be offered here. Struggle, transformation, and conversion are essential ingredients, however. The ancient struggle of Jacob with God is a powerful statement of the steward's struggle:

> The story of Jacob's God-wrestle, recorded in Genesis 32, . . . is a story of pain and transformation. In our judgment that is exactly what the future holds. It is a tale for the American church. It holds with equal force for the American people as a whole, at least for those outside the ranks of the very poor.[11]

The biblical record indicates that Jacob had cheated his brother Esau out of his birthright. Then he had deceived his father Isaac in order to steal Esau's blessing. When Esau swore to kill his brother, Jacob left the land and lived estranged from his brother.

While apart Jacob had prospered and acquired abundant

9. George A. Lindbeck, "A Battle for Theology," in *Against the World for the World*, eds. Peter Berger and Richard Neuhaus, p. 30, as cited by Birch and Rasmussen in ibid., p. 71.

10. Ibid., pp. 71-72.

11. Ibid., p. 74.

goods and slaves, living a self-serving life. He continued to be the strong one who bent things to his own ends.

Such abundance was not enough, however. He remained estranged from his brother. He knew that he could never be whole until he returned and was reconciled with his brother Esau.

The journey back was a risk because he did not know how his brother felt. On the last night of the return trip, Jacob spent the night alone on the banks of the river Jabbok. As night set in, Jacob was seized by a man who wrestled with him to the breaking of dawn. Jacob had always been in control before, and he wanted to be in control of this situation. Gradually, he began to realize that what he was wrestling was no less than the active presence of God. When Jacob knew, finally, that he could no longer be in control, the visitor blessed him. He was humbled and his thigh thrown out of joint.

The night visitor gave Jacob a new name—*a new identity*. He limped away a changed man, no longer Jacob, the one out for himself at the expense of his brother, but Israel, a name that pointed to a wider community of responsibility and bore God's promise. In recognition that his struggle had been with God, he named the place Peniel, "face of God," because there he saw God "face to face" (Genesis 32:30).

> Times of epochal transitions are times of the God-wrestle. God in human form seizes us unexpectedly. The struggle continues through a long night. It comes in the form of challenges and crises we did not elect and would not have chosen; like Jacob, however, we did much to create them. Through them God confronts us, often in the form of the antagonist. Yet only there, in the God-wrestle, does transformation occur. Only in a struggle he did not elect does Jacob receive a new identity and become Israel. It is not without pain. And it is not *without injury* (emphasis added).[12]

12. Ibid., p. 75.

The Journey

The struggle and the pain of wrestling with God are the essential ingredients of the process through which a steward is born. In some way, the steward's body or life will bear the marks of the struggle. The Christian steward walks with a limp!

This book has portrayed the life of the Christian steward and the church as a journey. Though the journey has been described as a series of steps, you should not assume that the steps must necessarily occur in the precise order that they occur in this book. Nor should it be assumed that a step once taken need never be repeated. The journey is not entirely predictable; many unexpected twists and turns await you. Just when you think you have figured out the journey, a new development is almost certain to take place. That is part of the adventure of journeying with God. Struggle, pain, and transformation are necessary if identity as steward is to emerge.

Your continuing journey as a steward of God will involve growth and change as God leads you. It may mean a wrestling with God. It may mean a radical change in the way you perceive the reality of the world of which you are a part. It may mean a change in your life-style, in the way in which you are accustomed to doing things.

It may mean being "a stranger, an exile, an alien, seeking to sing the Lord's song in a strange land."[13] To contemplate this is to be frightened and exhilarated at the same time. But to engage in such a journey of faith is to be a steward of God!

13. Jim Wallis, *Agenda for Biblical People: A New Edition* (San Francisco: Harper & Row, 1984), p. 29.

Questions and Suggestions
for Individual Reflection and Action

1. Reflect on the ways in which you have grown and changed in your journey as a Christian steward while reading *Stepping Stones of the Steward*. Have the experiences of prayer, study, reflection, and action left a mark on you? Do you "walk with a limp"? In what ways?

2. How can you continue to grow and to change? How can you be supportive of others in their journeys as stewards, particularly when someone is "walking with a limp"? How can you receive support for your journey?

3. Review the entire plan that you have been developing. What changes need to be made? What persons do you need to contact? Above all, continue times of prayer and study. The journey of the Christian steward is ongoing.

Study Guide

Introduction

Stepping Stones of the Steward can be used in a number of ways:

- Lay study groups in a congregation;
- Individual study[1];
- Preaching resource by pastors;
- Retreat or conference setting;
- Sunday church school elective study[2]; and
- Resource for stewardship leaders.

This study guide is designed to encourage and facilitate group use of *Stepping Stones of the Steward*. There are benefits for an individual reading a book. Those benefits can be enhanced, however, when the implications of the book are translated into

1. Questions and suggestions for individual reflection and action have been drawn, in part, from this study guide and placed at the end of each chapter.

2. The 15-session design can be modified to a 13-session design for Sunday church school elective study by asking participants to read the Introduction and Chapter 1 prior to the first session, and by selecting activities from the first two sessions and using them in the first session. In a similar manner, selected activities from Sessions 6 and 7 (related to resources) can be combined into one session.

the reality of an actual situation through the dynamics and cross-fertilization of a small group process. It is my hope that groups in your church will use this book to study, reflect, pray, and struggle together with actual issues in your congregation.

For the purpose of flexibility, *two designs* are presented: *a fifteen-session design* and *a five-session design.* (See Note 2 on page 163 for a suggested modification to make the fifteen-session design into a design for thirteen sessions.) Each session is designed for sixty minutes, though the sessions can be expanded easily if more time is available. The fifteen-session design uses the introduction and each of the other fourteen chapters of the book. The five-session design uses the introduction and each of the four parts of the book. The fifteen-session design has the advantages of allowing a more detailed and experiential process and providing opportunity to formulate and make recommendations to the congregation. The choice as to which design you use will depend upon your situation and the number of sessions available. The leader(s) will need to be selected ahead of time to facilitate the study process.

Each participant will need to read the sections indicated in preparation for each session.

It will often be suggested that thoughts and ideas be placed on newsprint. This allows those thoughts and ideas to be put "up front" where they can be seen by each participant. It is also easy to keep the newsprint to display those ideas in another setting or to transcribe the ideas onto 8 1/2" x 11" paper.

It is my hope that your journey as a Christian steward will be enabled as you participate in a study group.

Ronald E. Vallet

FIFTEEN-SESSION DESIGN

Session 1

All participants should read the book's Introduction prior to this first session.

Materials Needed: Newsprint sheets, markers, masking tape.

1. In threes or fours, share your understandings of stewardship as a child, as a youth, and at this time in your life. (15 minutes)

2. Working individually, each person draws or writes something on a sheet of newsprint that depicts his or her present understanding of stewardship. (10 minutes)

3. Each person displays his or her newsprint sheet and comments briefly about what is on the newsprint. (15 minutes)

4. Place on newsprint the responses of members of the group to this question: "What is your response to the holistic view of stewardship presented in the Introduction and particularly the statement that 'While the church engages in mission, it is the identity of the Christian (and the church) as steward that is the more fundamental category'?" (10 minutes)

5. Discuss and place on newsprint what it means to conceive the life passage of the Christian as the "journey of a Christian steward." (10 minutes)

Assignment: Each participant should read Chapter 1: "Love That Just Won't Quit" prior to the next session. NOTE: Newsprint notes from this and subsequent sessions should be saved for consolidation and use in Session 14.

Session 2

Materials Needed: Newsprint sheets, markers, masking tape.

1. Discuss and place on newsprint the group's responses to these questions: "What is the climactic scene in the parable of the prodigal father?" "Why?" "What is the essential point of the parable of the prodigal father?" "Why do you think the author used this name for the parable?" (15 minutes)

2. With everyone sitting in a circle, lead the participants in Group Conversation, giving those who wish to do so an opportunity to share an experience (not an opinion) that was brought to mind by the parable of the prodigal father. Remind participants that Group Conversation is not to be confused with group discussion, which is problem-and-intellect centered. Group Conversation is person-and-feeling centered. (15 minutes)

3. In threes or fours, discuss the advantages and disadvantages of conceiving the first stepping stone of the journey of the Christian steward as a realization of the reality of God's love. "Why is this starting point not the only 'stepping stone' in the Christian steward's journey?" (10 minutes)

4. Working as a total group, discuss and place on newsprint the group's responses to these questions: "What are the similarities and differences in the two brothers' relationship to their father?" "What does this say about how much God loves you?" (20 minutes)

Assignment: Each participant should read Chapter 2: "Joy That Endures" prior to the next session. Be prepared to share an experience of joy that you experience or observe between now and the next session.

Session 3

Materials Needed: Newsprint sheets, markers, masking tape, space for role playing.

1. Give each participant an opportunity to share an experience of joy that he or she experienced or observed since the last session. (15 minutes)

2. Ask members of the group to role play the parable of the lost sheep or the lost coin. Give participants and observers opportunity to share their feelings. (15 minutes)

3. In threes or fours, discuss where you see evidences of joy in your life, in the lives of members of your congregation, and in the corporate life of your congregation. Can you identify the sources of the joy you have observed? (15 minutes)

4. Discuss and place on newsprint the group's responses to this question: "Why is joy an essential ingredient in the experience of the Christian steward?" (15 minutes)

Assignment: Each participant should read Chapter 3: "Your Response to God: A Multiple Choice" prior to the next session. Read and be prepared to share newspaper or news magazine accounts that illustrate a choice that someone was faced with and the decision that was made. Also, be prepared to share "A Time I Didn't Listen to God" in a small group setting.

Session 4

Materials Needed: Newsprint sheets, markers, masking tape.

1. Give each participant an opportunity to share a news account that illustrates a choice that confronted someone and the decision that he or she made. (15 minutes)

2. To practice listening skills, divide the group into triads (groups of three), with participants in each triad designating themselves A, B, or C. In each group, one person acts as referee and the other two as participants in a discussion of "A Time I Didn't Listen to God." One will be the speaker and the other the listener. Give the following instructions:

A. Participant A begins as speaker; participant B as listener; and participant C as referee.

B. Participant A speaks for three minutes. Participant B then takes two minutes to summarize in his or her own words what has been said. Participant A confirms the accuracy (or inaccuracy) of the listener's feedback. The referee may interrupt to help clear up any misunderstanding.

C. The roles are changed and the process repeated until each person has taken each role. (15 minutes)

3. Discuss and place on newsprint the group's responses to this question: "Why is it difficult (or not difficult) to 'listen' to and respond to God?" "What are some of the helping and blocking factors?" (15 minutes)

4. Discuss and place on newsprint the group's responses to this question: "What are some specific arenas of action about which you and your congregation need to 'listen' and respond to God?" (15 minutes)

Assignment: Each participant should read Chapter 4: "A Purpose That Attracts" prior to the next session. Practice listening skills by asking two or three members of your church (who are not in this study group), "What do you feel is the main purpose of our church?" Be prepared to share the responses at the next session.

Session 5

Materials Needed: Newsprint sheets, markers, masking tape.

1. Give each participant an opportunity to share the responses he/she received to the question, "What do you feel is the main purpose of our church?" Record the responses on newsprint. (15 minutes)

2. In threes or fours, respond to these questions: "Do you sometimes leave God out of the equation when thinking about your purpose in life?" "Why or why not?" (15 minutes)

3. Discuss and place on newsprint the group's responses to this question: "Are there ways in which you behave as the children in the parable—arguing with no clear sense of purpose?" "What are they?" (15 minutes)

4. In threes or fours, share with one another the extent to which you feel yourself to be a Christian steward. What is helping or hindering you at this time? (15 minutes)

Assignment: Each participant should read Chapter 5: "God Is Ready to Provide Resources" prior to the next session. Prepare (on newsprint if possible) a list of resources that God makes available to you and your congregation. Be prepared to post the list at the next session.

Session 6

Materials needed: Newsprint sheets, markers, masking tape.

1. Ask each participant to post the list of resources that God makes available to him or her and to the congregation. Each person walks around and silently reads the other lists. (15 minutes)

2. In threes or fours, respond to these questions: "Are there resources God wants to make available to you and our congregation that are not on the lists?" "If so, what are they?" (15 minutes)

3. Discuss and place on newsprint the group's responses to these questions: "In what ways is God like or not like the neighbor in the parable?" "What are your feelings about the 'utter availability' of God as expressed in the chapter?" (15 minutes)

4. Discuss and place on newsprint the group's responses to these questions: "Do you and/or our congregation as Christian stewards sometimes squander the benefit of God's greatest gift—Jesus the Christ?" "In what ways?" (15 minutes)

Assignment: Each participant should read Chapter 6: "Accepting God's Resources" prior to the next session. Thinking about God's purpose for you and for your congregation, prepare (on newsprint if possible) a list of "missing" resources needed to carry out those purposes. Be prepared to post the list at the next session. Also, bring a penny, a nickel, a dime, and a quarter to the session.

Session 7

Materials Needed: Newsprint sheets, markers, masking tape.

1. Ask each participant to post the list of "missing" resources needed to carry out God's purpose for him/her and for the congregation. Each person walks around and silently reads the other lists. (10 minutes)

2. Compile a summary of the lists on newsprint and test for group consensus. Discuss these questions for each resource listed, "Why haven't we been willing or able to accept this resource from God?" "What would we need to do differently to be able to accept this resource?" (15 minutes)

3. Participate in giving and receiving coins.[3] Before beginning, the leader should caution the group that comments will be limited to the person offering a coin, accepting a coin, or sharing feelings of rejection. If there are more than fifteen persons, divide into smaller groups of approximately eight to ten persons.

A. Each person is asked to select from the four coins each brought the one that seems most appropriate as representing himself or herself. Possible basis might be size, utility, value, inscriptions, or composition.

B. Each participant silently makes an emotional commitment to give that one coin to another member of the group. Stress that participants may not later change their commitment either to reciprocate or compassionately to include another member. Participants may not present their coin to the group as a whole.

C. Each participant in turn presents the coin chosen, representing a part of himself/herself, to the member of the group he or she has selected. The presentation should be made in the first person, stressing eye contact. The process moves clockwise.

3. Adapted from J. William Pfeiffer and John E. Jones, A *Handbook of Structured Experiences for Human Relations Training*, vol. 1, rev. ed. (Iowa City, IA: University Associates Press, 1972), pp. 113-14.

D. Beginning with the participant who received the most coins and then to all other participants who received coins, each receiver will share with the group his/her feelings about receiving the gift. The comments should be directed to the giver and may include such items as unexpected gifts and the receiver's analysis of why he or she received the gift.

E. Participants who did not receive coins are now asked to respond. This should be preceded by a brief comment that rejection, however slight, is one of the most difficult emotional reactions with which to deal. (25 minutes)

4. Discuss and put on newsprint the group's responses to these questions: "How does the 'coin process' differ from accepting resources from God who wants to provide all the resources you and our congregation need?" "How can you accept the resources that God wants to provide?" (10 minutes)

Assignment: Each participant should read Chapter 7: "What Are Your Talents?" prior to the next session. Prepare a list of the talents you feel God has entrusted to you and be prepared to post the list at the next session. Be as honest and realistic as possible. The group leader should bring fresh lemons (one for each person) to the next session.

Session 8

Materials Needed: Newsprint sheets, markers, masking tape, one lemon for each participant.

1. Ask each participant to post the list of his or her talents prepared for this session. Each person walks around and silently reads the lists. (10 minutes)

2. In threes or fours, identify the talents of each person. This may include affirmation of what was posted and may also include talents that were not on that person's list. (15 minutes)

3. Ask the participants to sit in a large circle and distribute a lemon to each person, explaining that no two lemons are alike.[4] Ask each person to take three minutes to "become acquainted" with his or her lemon. Place all the lemons in a container (such as a paper bag) and mix well. Then have each person take a lemon (any lemon) out of the container. Each person passes the lemon to the right, examining each one in order to identify his or her own. When a lemon is identified, it is placed in the owner's lap and other lemons are passed until each person has his or her lemon. Ask for group discussion of the statement, "Just as each lemon is unique, with no two alike, so each person is unique. God has entrusted a unique set of talents, skills, and abilities to each person." Encourage each person to keep and use his or her lemon in a special way (lemonade, lemon pudding cake, lemon pie, to give to someone, etc.) that will help him/her remember this experience and learning. (20 minutes)

4. Discuss and place on newsprint the group's responses to this question: "In light of the parable, how is the Christian steward held accountable for use of the talents, abilities, and skills that God has entrusted to him/her?" (15 minutes)

Assignment: Each participant should read Chapter 8: "Your Money or Your Life!" prior to the next session. Explain that each person will have the opportunity to participate (or not to participate) in a "pocketbook probe."

4. Adapted from ibid., vol. 3 (1971), pp. 102-3.

Session 9

Materials Needed: Newsprint sheets, markers, masking tape.

1. Ask the group to divide into three parts, as follows[5]:

A. Those persons willing to have their pocketbook, wallet, purse, or checkbook examined by others;

B. Those persons unwilling to have their pocketbooks examined but who are willing to examine others'; and

C. Those unwilling to do either.

The purpose is to explore feelings when "your" money and possessions are explored and examined by someone else, or when you check out money and possessions that "belong" to someone else. Members of group B examine the pocketbooks of group A, with group C observing. Talking is encouraged. When the examination period is over (10 minutes) give participants opportunity to share their feelings. Ask questions such as: "Why did you choose to be in the group you chose?" "What were your feelings during the examination?" (20 minutes)

2. Discuss and place on newsprint the group's response to this question: "In light of the parable and if God is owner of 'your' money, what does that say about your life-style and how you make financial decisions?" (20 minutes)

3. Discuss and place on newsprint the group's responses to this question: "In light of the parable and if God is owner of the money given in the weekly offerings to our congregation, how should our church set priorities and make budgetary and financial decisions?" (20 minutes)

Assignment: Each participant should read Chapter 9: "Risk Taking" prior to the next session. Be prepared to respond to these questions: "What is the greatest risk that you or your family ever took?" "What is the greatest risk our congregation ever took?"

5. Adapted from ibid., vol. 2 (1970), p. 98.

Session 10

Materials Needed: Newsprint sheets, markers, masking tape.

1. In threes or fours, discuss the questions assigned at the previous session: "What is the greatest risk that you or your family ever took?" "What is the greatest risk our congregation ever took?" (15 minutes)

2. Discuss and place on newsprint the group's responses to this question: "In light of the parable and as a Christian steward, what, if anything, is worth your risking everything for?" (20 minutes)

3. Discuss and place on newsprint the group's responses to this question: "As a steward of the gospel, what risks can/should our congregation be willing to take?" "For what purpose should these risks be taken?" "What recommendations might this group make?" (25 minutes)

Assignment: Each participant should read Chapter 10: "Caring for Others" prior to the next session. If any recommendations came out of Step #3, the leader and/or other designated members of the group should plan how to follow through in the appropriate way in your congregation. NOTE: In session 14, any recommendations that emerge from this will be coordinated.

Session 11

Materials Needed: Newsprint sheets, markers, masking tape.

1. In threes or fours, respond to this question: "In your community, who is the neighbor, the 'other,' to whom you as a Christian steward are to reach out?" (15 minutes)

2. Each smaller group shares with the total group and responses are placed on newsprint and consolidated. (10 minutes)

3. Discuss and place on newsprint the group's responses to the following: "What specific ministries of outreach into the community should our congregation undertake?" "What steps would have to be taken?" "What resources would be needed?" "What recommendations might this group make?" (35 minutes)

Assignment: Each participant should read Chapter 11: "Getting What You Deserve" prior to the next session. Follow through on any recommendations as suggested in the assignment at the end of Session 10.

Session 12

Materials Needed: Newsprint sheets, markers, masking tape.

1. Ask members of the group to role-play the parable of the laborers in the vineyard. Consider doing the "North American" version found in Chapter 11. Give participants and observers opportunity to share their feelings. (10 minutes)

2. In threes and fours, discuss these questions: "How do you respond to the concept that God gives people what they need, not what they deserve?" "Is this 'justice'?" (15 minutes)

3. Discuss and place on newsprint the group's responses to this question: "How can we, as Christian stewards, follow God's example of reaching out in an uncalculating love?" (15 minutes)

4. Discuss and place on newsprint the group's responses to this question: "How would the ministry of our congregation be different if we adopted a life-style of receiving and giving uncalculated love?" "What steps would have to be taken?" "What resources would be needed?" "What recommendations might this group make?" (20 minutes)

Assignment: Each participant should read Chapter 12: "Care for the Earth and Beyond" prior to the next session. Look for and be prepared to share newspaper or news magazine accounts that portray problems and/or solutions related to the Earth and its finite resources. Follow through on any recommendations as suggested in the assignment at the end of Session 10.

Session 13

Materials Needed: Newsprint sheets, markers, masking tape.

1. Give each participant an opportunity to share a news account related to the earth and its finite resources. (15 minutes)

2. In threes or fours, discuss these questions: "Does 'turf protection' take place in your life and in the life of our congregation?" "If so, in what ways?" (10 minutes)

3. Discuss and place on newsprint the group's responses to this question: "How can you, as a Christian steward, respond meaningfully to the finite limits of resources on the earth?" (15 minutes)

4. Discuss and place on newsprint the group's responses to these questions: "Recognizing that 'the earth is the Lord's,' what practical steps can our congregation take to address and help resolve problems related to care for the earth?" "What resources would be needed?" "What recommendations might this group make?" (20 minutes)

Assignment: Each participant should read Chapter 13: "Shrewdness: Assessing Reality" prior to the next session. Acting on behalf of the group, someone should consolidate and place on newsprint all recommendations from this and earlier sessions.

Session 14

Materials Needed: Newsprint listing the group's recommendations, newsprint sheets, markers, masking tape.

1. Display the newsprint sheets from Session 12 that consolidate the group's recommendations. Review the recommendations (and newsprint from other sessions as needed), making sure that they reflect fairly the group's work in earlier sessions. (15 minutes)

2. In threes or fours, discuss these questions: "Why are Christians sometimes charged with not having 'common sense'?" "Are the charges justified?" "If so, in what way?" (10 minutes)

3. Discuss and place on newsprint the group's responses to the following: "How can our congregation engage in stewardship that combines 'shrewdness' and caring love?" Again, review the recommendations and agree on those that the group wishes to make to other persons or groups in the church. Include answers to the following: "What are we recommending?" "What resources would be required?" "When and to whom should the recommendations be made?" "Who should act on our behalf?" (35 minutes)

Assignment: Each participant should read Chapter 14: "Growth and Change" prior to the next session. Reflect on and be prepared to share ways in which you have grown and changed since the first session. In other words, "How has your journey gone?" Follow through on the group's recommendations as decided.

Session 15

Materials Needed: Newsprint sheets, markers, masking tape.

1. In threes and fours, share with one another ways in which you have grown and changed during your journey as a Christian steward since the first session. "Do you 'walk with a limp'?" (15 minutes)

2. Discuss and place on newsprint the group's responses to the following: "How can we, in our journeys as Christian stewards, continue to grow and to change?" "How can we be supportive of one another in our journey as stewards, particularly when someone is 'walking with a limp'?" (20 minutes)

3. Discuss and place on newsprint the group's responses to this question: "How can we help others experience the joys and challenges of the journey of the Christian steward?" (20 minutes)

4. In a circle, with hands joined, participate in prayer. Each person can be invited to offer a sentence prayer expressing thanks for the journey and asking God's help as the journey continues. (5 minutes)

FIVE-SESSION DESIGN

Session 1

All participants should read the book's Introduction prior to this first session.

Materials Needed: Newsprint sheets, markers, masking tape.

1. In threes or fours, share your understandings of stewardship as a child, as a youth, and at this time in your life. (15 minutes)

2. Working individually, each person draws or writes something on a sheet of newsprint that depicts his or her present understanding of stewardship. (10 minutes)

3. Each person displays his or her newsprint sheet and comments briefly about what is on the newsprint. (15 minutes)

4. Place on newsprint the responses of members of the group to this question: "What is your response to the holistic view of stewardship presented in the Introduction and particularly the statement that 'While the church engages in mission, it is the identity of the Christian (and the church) as steward that is the more fundamental category'?" (10 minutes)

5. Discuss and place on newsprint what it means to conceive the life passage of the Christian as the "journey of a Christian steward." (10 minutes)

Assignment: Each participant should read Part I: "Gaining a Sense of Purpose" (Chapters 1, 2, 3, and 4) prior to the next session. Be prepared to share an experience of joy that you experience or observe between now and the next session. NOTE: Newsprint notes from this and other sessions should be saved for consolidation and use in later sessions.

Session 2

Materials Needed: Newsprint sheets, markers, masking tape.

1. In threes or fours, discuss the advantages and disadvantages of conceiving the first stepping stone of the journey of the Christian steward as a realization of the reality of God's love (Chapter 1) and why joy (Chapter 2) is an essential ingredient in the experience of the Christian steward. (20 minutes)

2. Place on newsprint and discuss the responses of the groups of threes and fours. (10 minutes)

3. Discuss and place on newsprint the group's responses to these questions: "Related to Chapter 3, 'Why is it difficult (or not difficult) to listen to and respond to God?'" "What are some of the helping and blocking factors?" (15 minutes)

4. Discuss these questions: "Are there ways in which you behave as the children in the parable (Chapter 4) —arguing with no clear sense of purpose?" "What are they?" (15 minutes)

Assignment: Each participant should read Part II: "Using Resources and Taking Risks" (Chapters 5, 6, 7, 8, and 9) prior to the next session. Prepare (on newsprint if possible) a list of resources that God makes available to you and your congregation. Be prepared to post the list at the next session.

Session 3

Materials Needed: Lists of resources, newsprint sheets, markers, masking tape.

1. Ask each participant to post the list of resources that God makes available to him or her and to the congregation. Each person walks around and silently reads the other lists. (10 minutes)

2. As a total group, discuss feelings and responses to the lists of resources. (10 minutes)

3. Discuss and place on newsprint the group's responses to these questions: "What are the life-style implications if you and other members of our congregation recognize and acknowledge God as Creator and Owner and are willing to accept resources as being from God?" (Chapters 5 and 6) and "How is the Christian steward held accountable for use of the talents, abilities, skills, and money that God has entrusted to him/her?" (Chapters 7 and 8). (20 minutes)

4. Discuss and place on newsprint the group's responses to these questions: "Related to Chapter 9, as a steward of the gospel, what risks can/should our congregation be willing to take?" "For what purpose should these risks be taken?" "What recommendations might this group make?" (20 minutes)

Assignment: Each participant should read Part III: "Reaching Out" (Chapters 10, 11, and 12). Look for and be prepared to share newspaper or news magazine accounts that portray problems and/or solutions related to the earth and its finite resources.

Session 4

Materials Needed: News accounts related to the earth and its resources, newsprint sheets, markers, masking tape.

1. In threes or fours, respond to this question related to Chapter 10: "In your community, who is the neighbor, the 'other,' to whom you as a Christian steward are to reach out?" (15 minutes)

2. Each smaller group shares with the total group and responses are placed on newsprint. Discuss together. (10 minutes)

3. Discuss and place on newsprint the group's responses to this question: "How can we, as Christian stewards, follow God's example of reaching out in an uncalculating love?" (Chapter 11). (15 minutes)

4. Related to Chapter 12, give each participant an opportunity to share a news account related to the earth and its finite resources. Discuss and place on newsprint the group's responses to these questions: "Recognizing that 'the earth is the Lord's,' what practical steps can our congregation take to address and help resolve problems related to care for the earth?" "What resources would be needed?" "What recommendations might this group make?" (20 minutes)

Assignment: Each participant should read Part IV: "Reality and Growth" (Chapters 13 and 14) prior to the next session. Reflect on and be prepared to share ways in which you have grown and changed since the first session. In other words, "How has your journey gone?"

Session 5

Materials Needed: Newsprint sheets, markers, masking tape.

1. In threes or fours, discuss these questions: "Why are Christians sometimes charged with not being shrewd?" "Are the charges justified?" "If so, in what way?" (Chapter 13). (10 minutes)

2. Each smaller group shares with the total group and responses are placed on newsprint. Discuss together. (5 minutes)

3. Discuss and place on newsprint the group's responses to the following: "How can our congregation engage in stewardship that combines 'shrewdness' and caring love?" Review the recommendations from Session 3 and agree on those that the group wishes to make to other persons or groups in the church. Include answers to the following: "What are we recommending?" "What resources would be required?" "When and to whom should the recommendations be made?" "Who should act on our behalf?" (20 minutes)

4. In threes and fours, share with one another ways in which you have grown and changed during your journey as a Christian steward since the first session (Chapter 14). "Do you 'walk with a limp'?" (10 minutes)

5. Discuss and place on newsprint the group's responses to the following: "How can we, in our journeys as Christian stewards, continue to grow and to change?" "How can we be supportive of one another in our journey as stewards, particularly when someone is 'walking with a limp'?" (10 minutes)

6. In a circle, with hands joined, participate in prayer. Each person can be invited to offer a sentence prayer expressing thanks for the journey and asking God's help as the journey continues. (5 minutes)